Surviving a Hero

A Therapist Looks At Family Loss

By

Catherine Carroll-Parker, Ph.D., M.S.W.

This book is a work of non-fiction. Names and places have
been changed to protect the privacy of all individuals. The
events and situations are true.

ISBN: 1-4107-5794-3 (e-book)
ISBN: 1-4107-5793-5 (Paperback)

Library of Congress Control Number: 2003094105

This book is printed on acid free paper.

Printed in the United States of America
Bloomington, IN

1stBooks – rev. 6/18/03

"GREATER LOVE HAS NO MAN
THAN THIS,

THAT HE LAY DOWN HIS LIFE FOR
HIS FRIENDS."

(John 15:13, The Holy Bible)

I never met my paternal grandfather. He was a New York City Fireman and was killed in the line of duty in a Hunts Point fire eighteen years before my birth. I never met my maternal grandfather either. He also was in the FDNY, but survived to retire. He died three years before I was born.

I did get to meet my father, though. Like the rest of the males in the family, he too worked for the Fire Department of the City of New York. He died in a Bronx fire when I was three years old with five of his comrades.

Many years have passed since that happened. In my family, lives have been lived and lost, and had my father survived he would have had quite a time keeping up with his four children and later, his eleven grandchildren. He would have had plenty of advice, I'm sure, for my own son who became a soldier and police officer. I can imagine my father regaling him with his own war stories over some drinks at a bar, tapping the back of the barstool as he did (for emphasis), and laughing uproariously at his own jokes. He would have won their love and earned their respect. He was just that kind of guy...Had he lived.

I can see him looking very proud at the graduations of his children, and maybe even making a sideways comment about my choice to become a psychologist. He would have believed that there was nothing that couldn't be solved by either a big swat or a bigger laugh. That's the way he was…Had he lived.

But, he didn't make it that far. He died at the age of forty-one, and we have never stopped missing him. With all his flaws, he was our hero. This book is for all of the heroes. All those who ever walked into danger. All those that gave everything they had for people they knew, and people they didn't. For all of those men and women that are now and always will be, missed by families they left behind. By families that have carefully protected their medals and flags and memories. This book is for us, the children of these brave souls that often wished that they weren't so brave. Who would have preferred that they stayed with us much longer.

This book is for my family. For all the families. This book is for my father.

Catherine Carroll-Parker, MSW, Ph.D. 2003

CHAPTER ONE

April, 1956. With all of the changes that have taken place over the intervening years, all of the progress, and all of the lives lived, almost fifty years seems long indeed. And perhaps after all, it is. But for six families, the years have not gone as quickly or as easily as they had anticipated so long ago before that date ever came. Had someone asked them what they wished and saw for themselves in their futures prior to that time, they would have imagined for themselves a life of relative normalcy. A life in which fathers and mothers worked at their respective roles and raised their children. Where children grew to adulthood sharing a home with their parents and siblings, to later become decent men and women on their own. They would have told you that they expected the normal ups and downs of life but hoped for more ups, and that the thought of a future in a post-war world was positive and they looked forward to it. But that would have been before April 4, 1956. On that night in a neighborhood in the Bronx, those six families lives would veer off the course they had envisioned. And it would happen so quickly and

1

completely that they would later forget they had ever had a different dream for themselves. They would forfeit, in one moment of complete bravery or insanity, depending upon how you looked at it, their futures, their family units, their finances and their chances of ever again being shaped by something other than tragedy. On that night almost fifty years ago, six men of the services which sustained and protected their city would make a sacrifice that would resonate in the hearts and minds of their families forever. They would not be the first or the last to do so, certainly. But they would be our men and our sacrifice too. And although this is the story of one of these men and his family, it is a story for any family that has experienced the same awful reality of losing their husband or father in the course of his service to others.

It was a warehouse fire. The alarms were being sent across the Bronx summoning the fire companies to the blaze. At Engine Company 48, Fireman First Grade Edward Carroll was on the desk. He logged the time, the location, and the number of alarms. Four. Bigger than he expected. And close to the elevated train line. He signed the book as the fireman on watch, and then raced with the rest of the company to dress for the run. For a Wednesday night the call was unusual. And with this being the week after the Easter holiday, it was even more so. Most of the time after a holiday things were quiet, but apparently not tonight.

The men, all seasoned firefighters, were ready within seconds. They mounted the engine as they had a thousand times before, and sped off toward Third Avenue. It was early spring and for that, the guys on the back of the truck were thankful. Their ride would be more comfortable now that the weather was changing. It would probably be fair to say, even across all these years, that they were unprepared for what they saw when they reached the fire. The old movie theatre burned out of control. Trucks, hoses, captains, mayhem…And still the fire raged. The other companies that were already there were already trying to beat the flames back without success. Engine Company 48, their company, tumbled from the truck already in motion. Lieutenant Jack Malloy was already giving orders. Jack was the officer on duty tonight and well trusted by the men. They whipped the hoses from the wheels, and began the run toward the front of the building. Hellauer and Hanson grabbed the equipment and ladders and headed toward the entrance of the building, now obscured by the smoke. They knew the drill. They knew it was bad but they had faced

3

worse, and this one was not going to get any further away from them. The other men scattered in different directions grabbing more equipment, opening more hydrants. These men on duty tonight were veterans. They had worked together with the precision of years on the job, and they would do it again tonight.

The building was now an artificial flower factory in this latest incarnation. For more years than any of them could remember, it had been a movie theatre. No different from any of the old ones, it boasted a large marquis front held in place with massive chains on either side for support. The weight of that alone was horrendous, but the fire itself was an internal one burning wildly through the interior floors, fed by the chemicals the owners used for the plastic. The men looked at each other communicating their assessment without words. Building fires were always the worst, with infrastructures being complicated and uncertain, and the presence of chemicals always spelled the possibility of explosion. They knew it was bad. They knew from hours and months and years of experience and they knew that the only way to handle it was with total and absolute aggression. Hit it, isolate it, kill it, and do it as fast as possible. It wasn't rocket science, but it would require incredible skill…and guts. They had these from experience too.

These guys weren't short on courage. You couldn't do this job for years and not be able to summon up the fearlessness when you needed it. It was strange that way. They talked about it with each other. Not often, but sometimes after a close call in a fire someone would talk about the calm that came over them right at the moment when things took a turn for the worse. You weren't aware of it until you absolutely needed it, they said. The adrenaline would take over and become part of you, the one that you saved up all your strength in, the one that took over and let you…no, made you, really…go where minutes before would have horrified you. That's the way it was. And that's the way it had to be for you to do this job. It saved your life more than once, of that they were all certain.

Four of the guys went in. Hellauer, Hanson, Hoolan and Malloy. Hellauer and Hanson positioned the ladder on a diagonal to the wall. With Hanson steadying the base, Hellauer barreled up the ladder to the third rung nearest the top. Malloy and Hoolan were running the hoses to water down the walls, keeping the fire back at the base so the other two could work on the top. Carroll was at the entrance hauling more equipment and giving it water. But he was doing something else, too.

Ed Carroll was a fireman for eighteen years and was the son of a fireman killed in the line of duty years before. He was a smart guy, and no stranger to either fighting fire or building construction. He had a second job as a draftsman. He had graduated from Cooper Union College and had gone to St. John's Law School. He planned to retire into his own law practice after he retired from the department. With a practice and the pension, he could finally make things a little nice for his wife and family of four kids. One of his assignments on the job a few years ago had been building inspector. For that, you had to know construction and the hazards that went with it. He knew about structures and this one worried him. He scanned the front of the building and saw a barely discernible lean of the entry wall. He calculated the weight of the marquis as being about two tons or so, and tried to calculate the amount of strain that could be being put on the wall as the fire mangled its supports. Instinctively, he knew how bad that could be and how soon. It worried him with the same kind of urgency he had felt when a fire in the

South Bronx years ago had flashed unexpectedly and burned three firemen. The noise at the scene would have been distracting to anyone, but for now he was oblivious to it. He needed to talk to someone in charge, and there was just no time to lose. Stepping over the hoses, he scanned the helmets for the one he was looking for. There, by one of the trucks and off to the left side of the building, was the one he needed. The white helmet of the chief distinguished him from the firemen that were scrambling around the scene. Ed approached him and waited briefly for him to disengage from the other men to which he was reeling off rapid-fire orders. The chief nodded the go-ahead which meant for Carroll to state his business. The chief kept his eyes on the chaos, and watched for anything that would look like the latest tyranny of the moment. The tension was all over him. Carroll requested that the chief call the men out of the building. Not wait, but get them out now. He kept his eyes on the front wall as he talked.

"It's going to go, cap". There was no uncertainty in the way he said it. There was no uncertainty in him. Ed believed what he said. The chief paused, then looked at the building and gave his directive. It wasn't what Carroll had wanted to hear.

7

"We'll keep 'em in a few more minutes, then pull them".

And, that was it. He had made his decision, and would go with it. Ed Carroll knew that to argue would not only be futile, but would waste precious time. He was beginning to construct a plan. It would not be the chief's plan, certainly, but his alone. For the first time in eighteen years, he would purposefully not comply with the order of a superior. There were many times he had disagreed, and probably more times he had shaken his head at an order, but this felt different. There was an urgency he felt that he couldn't explain had someone asked him. He knew in his bones that the chief's "few more minutes" just might be too long. So he decided to act on his impulse. If he was wrong, he'd deal with that later. When they were safe.

He was moving now. Almost on automatic pilot. He glanced at the marquis again, sure it was leaning more forward. He quickened his pace looking for Ed Murphy, the driver of the truck for his house. Spotting him near the engine, he twisted something into his hand as he approached him. Standing with him now he reached for his wrist under the turnout coat and pulled at something.

"Ed," he said, "I'm going in to put up the call to run".

Ed Murphy had seen Carroll speaking with the chief.

"What did the chief say?" Murphy could tell from the activity and the men still running into the building that the chief had not yet issued the order to clear out. He'll still tell you today that he just didn't compute what was going on. He was caught up in the urgency or the moment, the noise, and the tension. He'd tell you with his voice still cracking that he wished he could have known.

Ed Carroll ignored the question, or at least that's what it seemed to Murphy.

Signaling for Murphy to open his hand, Carroll dropped two items into it.

"If I don't come out, give these to my family". With that, he turned and ran toward the entry door and disappeared into the building.

Murphy looked at the articles and saw a gold signet ring and an inexpensive watch. It had happened too fast for him to say anything. He watched the building. They would have the time to get out. It was tense, but the thing was still holding. Ed was just taking precautions but he'd make it out. Just like he always did. He slipped the jewelry into his pocket.

He heard Ed Carroll's shout to the men inside. He heard it, even above the deafening clamor of the scene. He would say later that really, that's all he heard. That yell that he knew was Carroll's, a few feet from the doorway. Just a few feet from the curb and the safety of the open street.

"GET OFF THE LADDERS! RUN FOR YOUR LIVES! GET OUT! IT"S GONNA GO!"

I can sometimes picture what could have happened inside that building. Ed may have grabbed one of the firemen, or spun around after he gave the warning. Hellauer and Hanson were startled from their concentrated efforts on the wall, and Hanson would have held the ladder to allow Hellauer to make his descent. Maybe Jack Malloy was still at the base of the ladder. They were racing, reacting to Carroll's alarm, though. Of that we're certain. We know that much by what we were told later.

They were running. All of them. They were within feet of being safe. Or if not safe, at least within feet of injuries that probably could have healed given time. They were moving toward the door when the marquis gave. When the marquis, weighing a couple of tons, finally reached the point where the wall to which it was attached could no longer support its weight. The wall was fractured by the blaze just enough and, more than enough, that all of the bulk of two tons of the marquis leaned toward the pavement with a screeching, cracking, deafening roar, and pulled the wall with it. The tons of brick and mortar and "used to be wall" slammed to the street with a force that blew the men outside off their feet and onto the middle of Third Avenue. The smoke that came from the collapse made visibility impossible. In only seconds, the structure had hit the ground, the noise was unbearable, and there were

11

impossibly huge mounds of concrete and rubble where a building had stood. Only moments before.

For a frozen mille-second that defied the ability to consciously process what had just happened, there was an equally deafening silence. For a brief instant, that seems to only happen after an unspeakable event, there was absolute quiet. It seemed that no one spoke or cried out or was capable of comprehending or expressing it. It was a moment of shock; horror, defeat, inevitability and disbelief all compressed into an instant of time. It was the sound of something that comes right before what you know is going to be one of the worst moments of your life, and you are powerless to anything but wait for it to hit you. You can't run, speak or hide. You can't duck and have it go by with only a close call. It's a sickening indefinable thing, and in the end, it will have your name on it.

And, there it was…Right there. Then came the most horrific noise a fireman could ever live to hear. Then came the cries of their brothers that were alive and trapped under those mounds. Muffled, anguished, and desperate. They were low, almost far away sounding. They were weak, is what they were exactly. The sounds were haunting, thready, and they were sounds that wounded people would make right before the pain rendered them unconscious. In an instant, firemen had shaken off the shock of the instants before. They leaped across burning metal and began to dig at the piles. Clawing. They strained at the concrete, displaced cinder blocks by tossing them. They took crowbars and pried the ones that they couldn't move. It took only minutes, but by then, the sounds had stopped. Undaunted, they dug with hands, poles…anything they could find. The price was too high not to. They could do nothing else. It took about half an hour. But never had any of those men experienced such long minutes. It was a slow and agonizing thirty minutes in which every one of them had to constantly fight the urge to scream in desperation as they labored to remove some of the impossible weight of the debris that littered the scene. They would have to focus, and refocus to get through it. And they did. In one half-hour they finally found them. Hellauer and Hanson were only a few feet apart. Malloy was over to the right as you faced the building. Carroll was only a few feet from the doorway and what could have been safety, had it happened just a little bit differently. Hoolan was farther back, probably closer to the wall by the time he started to run. Infasino was just outside the entrance to the building, but the bricks had landed on the street side, too. Six men. Six brothers had died at the scene, all in the process of trying to get out of the building. All running in response to Ed Carroll's call to get out. They knew they were running by the head injuries. To a man, they had had their leather helmets caved in at the back by the heavy bricks and mortar. They had been moving when they were hit and fast, because they were young, these men. All were from the same Engine Company…and Engine Company 48 from the Bronx was decimated. Only the driver, Ed Murphy remained to bring the truck back into the house that night of April 4, 1956.

As the ambulances took the bodies of the six brothers to Morissania Hospital in the Bronx, Fireman First Grade Edward Murphy drove the Engine back to his station alone. His grief would not overcome him yet. It was still too surreal, too raw. He was in shock. Too much for him to believe. He maneuvered the truck into its place, parked and dismounted from the engine. And then he heard it. There was a sort of metallic "jingling" noise coming from his coat. He put his hand in the pocket, drew out Eddie Carroll's ring and watch, and collapsed to the station floor in grief.

All of these men had families. Most with young children. Wives and sons and daughters and mothers and fathers that had no idea of what had happened...yet. Wives who put the kids to bed at their regular time, not knowing that not to far away their husbands, in the one brief instant they were given, were trying to run for their lives. Wives that were always leery of their husband's job, always afraid of the danger, and no matter what, did not want to be the survivor of a hero.

And, wives that were unaware that on this night in April, they already were.

CHAPTER TWO

Even before Ed Murphy rose from his crumpled position on the floor of the firehouse, New York reporters were contacting their papers with the story. Some of the press had been at the scene, getting the details of this big fire that was so hard to control. The Fire Department was dispatching chaplains and chiefs to the homes of the families, hoping to reach them before they saw the Late News on television. They wanted to be the ones to notify the survivors, and not have them learn of the deaths from the media. For the most part they succeeded but some confusion at the hospital would cause my family even more pain for a brief period. A miscommunication regarding my father's identity resulted in the retraction of the initial news of his death. The chaplain and chief were still at the apartment when a call came in to correct the news of his death. They said that it was Fireman "Charles" Carroll that was lost, not "Edward". And for a brief moment, although sorry for the other family, we allowed ourselves to breathe. My mother was beside herself with relief but less than an hour later, a second call corrected the first notification.

Unbelievably, they were correcting the correction. With profuse apologies, the dispatcher retracted his earlier phone call to verify that it was, in fact, Edward Carroll that lost his life and he was terribly sorry for any inconvenience this had caused. And just like that, we were left with the "inconvenience" beyond comprehension. Our father and my mother's husband of many years would never come home again. You could almost hear our lives shatter.

The New York newspapers headlined the tragedy the next day, and for many days to follow. It was labeled the worst loss to the Fire Department in decades. Six firefighters had died in a Bronx blaze. Six widows and nineteen children survived them. Stories detailed the careers and personal lives of the heroes, and my family members were interviewed for the human interest articles. As both the wife and mother of slain firemen, my grandmother was sought out for a feature story. She was too distraught at the time of the interview though, and a more distant family member spoke to the press as her representative. The men were called "heroes", "valiant", and "courageous". They were acknowledged for giving the supreme sacrifice. Their names were listed in most of the New York papers: Lieutenant John Malloy, Fireman

Frederick Hellauer, Fireman Arthur Hanson, Fireman William Hoolan, Fireman Charles Infasino, and Fireman Edward Carroll.

The city shrouded itself in mourning. Following the viewings of the men's bodies, a formal funeral took place in the heart of Manhattan. Caissons bearing the flag draped caskets would transverse Fifth Avenue, making the slow journey to St. Patrick's Cathedral. Hundreds of uniformed firefighters from across the nation would line the streets in homage to the slain six. Limousines carrying the bereaved family members snaked for miles behind the fire trucks bearing the bodies. In solidarity, the department once again demonstrated its reputation of "New York's Bravest". The funeral service was a testimony to the courage of the men whose caskets flanked the main altar. And when it was ended, each of the men was given a twenty one gun salute graveside. It was truly a hero's burial, reserved for those that had demonstrated superior bravery.

Following the funerals and the burials, and the press coverage given to the ensuing investigation of the fire, the city returned to normal. Of course, in recognition of the tragedy, building inspectors operated with heightened vigilance of chemical storage in the city's buildings. New regulations and codes were written to avoid a similar disaster. Services for the men continued but slowly, life took on its usual pace again. For all that is, except the survivors.

It's strange how the mind stores and recalls information. I remember a day when my brothers and sister were all seated in the living room, quiet except for the muffled sobbing each of them was doing. They were the picture of broken heartedness. I remember standing in the doorway of that room and for years, I thought that they were crying because a family dog had run away and not come home. I would hold that memory and that explanation of it until I realized that it was right after my father's death. It was him that they were mourning, united in suffering, and sharing silent tears. And that is exactly as our lives would develop. We would always be, and always have been, the macrocosm of that afternoon. We would be bound by a common grief, aware of our own and the other's pain, but silent about the depth and breadth of our loss.

We would have April of 1956 as a reference point for many of our feelings, behaviors and life choices. We all

19

would operate with an emotional void shaped like both loss and pride. In other words, we would be typical survivors of heroes.

On September 11, 2001, forty-five years after the Bronx blaze that took the life of my father and five of his fellow firefighters, another tragedy occurred. It made the event of 1956 pale in comparison if only by the sheer numbers and magnitude of the loss to the City of New York uniformed services. Over three hundred men would lose their lives in the horror of the collapse of the World Trade Centers. They too were doing the jobs that they had trained for, and loved. They, too, would walk into a building that would be the last place they would ever enter this side of eternity. The buildings, like the one in the Bronx so many years before, were in flames. The structure and integrity of its moorings was in imminent peril. Yet they went. Determined, fearful, brave...a myriad of contradictions perhaps. But, they went. And it was that act alone that made them heroes. At the end of that nightmare day, when acres of rubble, cement and girders lay strewn about the heart of Manhattan like broken leggos and alien movie set silhouettes, they had shrugged off the coil of mortal men and become heroes of incomprehensible courage to a heartbroken city. This time the size of the list of the dead and missing was staggering. Effectively, the Fire Department of the City of New York was almost decimated. The list of the casualties was not selective, political or status conscious. It claimed the brass of the department, long term veterans and rookies a month on the job with equal abandon. In one morning, in one insane, unprecedented act of horror, the worst had become the possible, and the possible had become reality.

I would be hard pressed to imagine that there would be anyone who was ever touched by the loss of anyone in the services that did not relive their own grief on September 11th. For me, years seemed to evaporate, and I resonated with the chest pain of some deep memory of personal loss. It was triggered by the sight of the devastation and the knowledge of such courage lost beneath the rubble. At the moment when your mind absorbs an event that even vaguely stirs something familiar to you, some primal response is triggered, and stirs the soul to groan in remembrance. And the child that was left behind, the one that you thought had been adequately comforted, once more looks out of your adult eyes with confusion and unprocessed tragedy.

Catherine Carroll-Parker, Ph.D., M.S.W.

I was only three years old when my father became a hero. And I was in my forties when the World Trade Center collapsed. The truth is, it didn't feel much different. The years evaporate and as you step up beside the brand new families of heroes and share their pain, your own comes with you. And the tears you shed in the present are mingled with those of the past.

CHAPTER THREE

I wanted to write this book for a few reasons of which no one is more important than the other. I wanted to tell the story of what could happen to the families of heroes, if they were unaware of the special dynamics and care was not taken. I wanted to tell my family's story as a prototype...almost as an example of how life after a tragedy can become almost stereotypical in its dysfunction if issues go unrecognized and untreated. Later they become the backdrop for larger problems, and if I could help a family avoid that, I would feel that I had accomplished something important. I wanted to tell the surviving adults about how difficult it is to grow up with an icon- an absent hero- and come out the other side unscathed. As a therapist, I wanted to apply the years of study, personal search and experience that I have gained through my own journey, to the task of making even one life better for the effort. I had wished for years that there had been some type of counsel or resource that my own family could have used way back before the scars deepened. Of course there were none, but there should have been.

Catherine Carroll-Parker, Ph.D., M.S.W.

If I had felt the motivation, I would have written this long ago as a study in dysfunctional families, but that was before September 11, 2001, and another war and I didn't feel the urgency. I feel that I have something to say to the survivors of those who have died in the service to others. First, I am the child of a New York City firefighter who was killed in the line of duty, and grew up in a family that experienced the tragedy and aftermath of that kind of loss. Second, I became a therapist, specializing in the area of Dysfunctional Families. Having an absent parent is a qualifier for that category. Of course, most families are dysfunctional. The products of imperfect people in relationship to each other. But families that experience the sudden and complete loss of a parent are particularly vulnerable. When that parent has died under heroic circumstances, the issues compound as the gamut of feelings become enmeshed and confused. The lost parent becomes larger than life and the survivors wrestle with acknowledging any negative feelings that they may have or have had involving them. I now think that my career choice was probably made as a child. I definitely know that I was looking for my own answers. I wanted to understand the aspects of the pain I felt down deep, and I knew that I had made many life decisions and manifested many behaviors as a result of being the child of a hero. I wanted to reclaim freedom of choice in my life. Choice to make decisions that did not emanate from an empty place at the dinner table or a need to recreate the past differently, but ones that were more informed by the present and relevant to my current needs and circumstances. I wanted to act out of a mindset of proaction rather than reaction. I wanted I suppose, to be free of the history that drove my decisions. Most of all, I was exhausted from my own misguided but understandable efforts to fix what had been so long ago broken. I became a very competent and insightful therapist because after my father's death, my role in the family was to fix emotional pain. But I'll get to that part later...

Then September 11th happened. The way that I reacted was almost primal. Unexpected intensity. It was the sheer horror of it certainly, but it was something else, too. There was a deep pain in my chest, the old pain of loss that I recognized as a familiar feeling of grief and it was back with ferocity. Years rolled back and the rubble in Manhattan became mixed with the rubble in the Bronx of so many years before.

Hundreds of men were trapped underneath concrete but whether hundreds or six, to me it felt the same. I cried for the widows and children. I mourned for the other victims too, but the kinship or the "kindredness" was with the widows and the children of the men that walked into death with fear covered in courage, when their sense of duty required nothing less. I mourned for the mothers, I grieved for the children, and then I cried for my own mother, my grandmother, my family and myself. I cried for the lost years when no one knew how to handle the consequences of an April night. I thought over all the mistaken explanations of our behaviors, all the life mistakes my family had made individually and collectively, and made a decision. That decision is this writing. If I could, I would tell whatever it took, including the sacred "family secrets" to the survivors of the World Trade tragedy, as well as any other person whose loved one lost their life in the name of honor. If I could, I would like to spare even one person from needless suffering in the wake of a loss that feels too big to bear. I would make suggestions as a child of a hero and as a therapist that would hopefully counteract some of the difficulties that surface in the course of surviving a hero. There are many writings that deal with tragedy. Certainly, there are books that address father loss, dysfunctional family systems, surviving a death and grieving. And in the reams of material written there is wise counsel. But the element that I have never seen in print deals with not only father loss, but that reality within the bigger context of the uniformed services or similar dangerous occupations. I refer to the brotherhood, if you will, of men that have chosen a career that inherently holds both danger and heroism and the possibility of giving their lives when those two elements merge. An occupation that so closely allies bravery and everyday work duties that it is distinguished among other careers. That group of men be they firefighters or policemen, or soldiers or rescue workers, share the elements of life and death every day of their work lives. So much so that there is closeness among them that few other career fields can equal. They become brothers in life, in work, and in death. Their wives become joined in camaraderie, too. Their unions are formed of pride, fear and a sense of belonging to a culture that is as old as there is need and as close as family. There is never a time when these women are not aware of the frailty of life. A day does not pass that they do not, at least fleetingly, consider the dangers of the job. But perhaps that is part of the reason that they love their men as they do. They have calculated the risk of possible loss, of receiving a dreaded visit by some chief of the Department or superior. These women and men have had to accept that reality if not with enthusiasm, than certainly with courage born of love. They have made a choice to accept the risks for the sake of the one who will take them. They have decided to love beyond their fears.

Anyway, I wanted to tell the story. I needed to apply whatever life and professional experiences I had gained to offer to those that were left in the same situation as we were, some resource. If experience is indeed the best teacher then perhaps mine will be of some help to those in the wake of their own personal loss.

Before that though, I would like to take you through the stories of my siblings and myself. Contained in them are classic roles that children of heroes often assume. They are identified as roles that occur in dysfunctional families as well, but don't let that reference discourage or insult you. I believe that by virtue of our humanity, we are all dysfunctional. We all have our traits and characteristics. We all have our weaknesses and penchants. What I refer to, and have first hand knowledge of, are the roles that we take to compensate for our loss. Or conversely, the ones we refuse because of the loss. It is that which makes the difference between health and dysfunction, really. The degree to which we react and how. In families that have lost a parent to heroism, there is a slightly different dynamic. The absent one can never be addressed and it feels disrespectful to admit (or have) any negative feelings. The one that survives becomes the focal point and life is skewed if only by the imbalance.

So allow me to take you into the home life of a family in an apartment in the Bronx in the years following the death of my father. I will bring us along quickly. Be sure to read between the lines.

CHAPTER FOUR

We lived in a two-bedroom apartment in the central Bronx, one block from Fordham Road. Back then, rents were low in keeping with the incomes of the times and the apartments themselves were older walk-ups with five stories. In the years before my father's death, my parents slept in the living room on a convertible couch and my brothers shared a bedroom, as did my sister and I. Quarters were tight but it was what we could afford, even with my father moonlighting with a drafting company. He was rarely home between working at the firehouse and his other job, but when he was, the house took on a different feel. He was the oldest of five brothers of Irish background which naturally made him a talker. He was a teaser as well, often setting us up with some accusation or another and then laughing when we howled in frustration. He was nothing if not social, and in conformity with his Irishness spent a good deal of his off time socializing and catching up on news with his friends at the local tavern. My mother hated that part. She would look for ways to catch him at this activity and when she invariably did, would get that pinched look on her face that was the signal of her great displeasure. It was the precursor to the verbal diatribe that always followed. It was the one thing that I remember my parents arguing about. It must have been fairly significant or at least often, because it made the impression on me that it did. When my father was supposed to go to the store to pick up some item for the household, he would take me along with him. I suppose the pull of the tavern was too difficult for him to resist because we always seemed to stop there first. He would sit me on the bar and I would entertain his friends with my precocious vocabulary which is a nice way of saying "smart mouth". He would buy me a coke with a cherry floating at the bottom which I just thought was the best thing you could get. I remember the smell of that bar to this day. The smell and how those men would throw back their heads and laugh. Most of them worked together. They might even have been hiding out from their wives too, now that I think of it. They were there for some down time and as always, hung out with their buddies from the job. He would be in his element, telling stories and entertaining with his quick wit and great delivery. They were great times. But then we would rush to the store with my father checking his watch and acting nervous. No sooner would we get home that my mother would pull me aside and ask me if we had made any stops. "Yes," I would say. "Daddy brought me for a soda". She of course, would have her antenna up. "And did the soda have a cherry in it?"

"Yes" I would say again, "it did."

How was I supposed to know that candy stores didn't serve sodas that way?

With that, she would swing her head in the direction of my father and he would look for all the world like the proverbial deer in the headlights. Despite his size he would appear to shrink right before our eyes and that would be it. She'd be off and running. I'd feel somehow guilty, and my father would conveniently remember that he had to leave right away for work at one job or the other. I wouldn't blame him either even though it was left to us to be party to my mother's verbal wind down as she stomped through the house. That always took longer than we hoped and took some of the fun out of my day. To make the point, I remember asking my sister when I could get a job too, and her laughing.

In all, I'd say that the tension that would arise between my father and mother had to do with his absences and the fact that she worried about him. She was concerned about his work in the Department, she worried that he pushed himself too hard, and I think it would be fair to say that she was weighed down under the responsibility of caring for us kids largely on her own. I think she resented his desire to be with his work buddies, thinking perhaps that they had the better part of his time and energies.

Nevertheless, they were married twenty-one years when he died. The long dance that they did with each other had survived eight pregnancies, five live births, one child's death, financial problems, family interference and his inevitable trips to the saloon when he was supposed to be getting groceries. Whatever the issues between them, whatever the reasons the tensions, they were committed. They had made a promise for better or worse, and if they experienced some of the worst, I believe they had also known much of the better with it.

My mother always told us a story after he was gone. That Easter she had made the traditional hard boiled eggs for the egg hunt. She had written all of our names on them and left them in the refrigerator once they had been found and turned into her for the nickels and dimes we got for finding them. On the day that my father died, she reached in and took an egg to eat. Inadvertently, she had eaten the egg

33

with my father's name on it and immediately felt uneasy. She would wonder later if she had experienced some type of premonition of something bad about to happen to him. She said that later that same day as she watched my father walk down the street en route to the firehouse, she saw him suddenly turn around and head back towards home. He came back to the apartment, climbing the three flights of stairs to kiss her goodbye saying that he had "forgot" and wanted to make sure that he did. Again she said later, she had the strange feeling if only by the total lack of precedence for his action. He had never turned and come back before. She would wonder if he too, felt a sense of foreboding and was taking the opportunity to settle matters for himself in the ways that he was able. She wondered if it was his way of saying "goodbye" should that be what would become his last gesture toward her.

I don't know. I didn't have any of those precognitions at the age of three so I can't say, but I wouldn't question it. I believed it was possible that he could have had some unconscious warning. I remember thinking that it was a frustrating story because if either of them had even thought that to be a possibility, they should have done something about it rather than wonder in respective silence. If she had really been that uneasy, why hadn't she stopped him? And if he felt something, no matter how vague, why didn't he stay when he came home to kiss her goodbye? But maybe those feelings weren't all that odd for either of them or maybe they each thought they were overreacting. I'll never have the answer for that. But those questions that I had came long after the events of April 4th, and the subject was moot anyway. I suppose that I was just trying to find some way that would have prevented his death from happening. In doing so, I once again revealed my own pain and anger that it did.

After the fire, my mother never slept in the convertible sofa again. She moved into the bedroom that my sister and I shared and slept with me. It was a very dysfunctional thing to do, actually. It had all the markings of being a need that she had and was extremely unhealthy from a psychological standpoint. Even in a situation like this a parent should not seek the comfort of or sleep with a child. But after his death, in some ways she became almost childlike herself and needed whatever emotional support that she thought her children could provide. When she first received the news that Wednesday night, she went into shock and couldn't remember if she had any family to contact. She summarily forgot about her own two brothers with whom she was fairly close, and my father's mother and four brothers. She regressed into a type of child, incapable of making a decision or giving information and stunned with the reality of being the surviving parent to four children. She leaned on her brother Phil, as she would for many years subsequent to that night. And she leaned on us. Especially as we got older. It was almost as if she transferred care and custody of her emotional wellbeing to the child that seemed most capable of caretaking at any given time. The custodians would change depending upon the situation, but it was the children that would become the parent, at least for the emotional and supportive tasks. The sole emotions that my mother seemed to be able to express were anger and fear, and those in significant quantities. Although not unusual for grieving persons to express those emotions initially as they pass through the grieving cycle, the anger gives way to the emotions that ultimately bring them through the process. I suspect that she never went past that initial phase and remained locked there throughout the years that followed.

When she knew on that night that she could not dismiss the finality through bargaining for my father's life, she entered into a state of anger that quite possibly kept her sane. She would use it as her strength, her defense mechanism, and her emotion of choice. In the first hours after my father's death was confirmed, that anger flared to the surface where it would stay. Her one directive at that time was not for her children, or the disposition of her husband's body, or those family members that needed to be notified. She turned her attention to my father's brothers and demanded that they not be the ones to go to my father's locker at the firehouse. With all of the mayhem of the moment, she took an adamant stand that was exclusionary and telling. She had long felt that his brothers had wronged her over the years of her marriage and at this moment, chose to make her stand. He was her husband, after all, and as his survivor she could finally overrule their wishes.

More of the same reaction surfaced during the three day viewing. She would speak of the inappropriate behavior of my father's mother, uncles and brothers at the viewing, claiming that one of his uncles had pushed her out of his way as he approached the casket. She was convinced it was because they blamed her for the necessity of his having to hold two jobs and was not able to see any faulty reasoning in this perspective. She was blatantly dismissing the fact that my father's joining the Fire Department had more to do with the death of his own father in the line of duty and was already in place when she met him, and that his taking a second job was due to finances and not her prompting. These things are what she chose to believe, however, against all wisdom and logic. So we left her to it knowing instinctively that she needed the strength her anger could lend her. She would sometimes vacillate between anger and helplessness and when under the sway of the latter, could be fairly immobilized. She was unable to make a decision, worried that it would be the wrong choice. She would let others make them for her but inevitably resent them for the ones they made. One such instance resulted in my brother and I being sent to relatives during the early weeks following my father's death. Of the many different houses that we were sent to, one belonged to an aunt who was known to be abusive. After she threatened me with a beating with a belt during my stay with her, I told my mother as soon as I got home. My mother immediately responded by both berating the family member that made the decision to send us there and threatening the responsible aunt with a law suit, or worse. Again, it was her anger that would surface to allow her to engage in the activities around her. It was the anger that kept her fear at bay. And so would it be in the future.

When the initial days and weeks were over and my brother and I returned home, it seemed that all of the solicitous relatives went back into their own lives. We were brought back to a home that was intrinsically and permanently altered, and somehow had to learn to adjust to life under unrecognizable circumstances. Occasionally visitors would still come, but it was very unlike the early days after the fire when it seemed our house was always filled with people. Some days, the wives of the other men would come to our apartment with their children and we would play with them as their mothers spent time talking with my mother. Firemen from my father's station house dropped in for coffee occasionally, but when they didn't, my mother isolated herself in the kitchen throughout the days and nights. This would become her place of refuge.

At dinner time when my mother would start to eat, she always would start to choke and grab my older brother's arm in panic. My poor brother would look horrified but eventually when she would be able to swallow again, dinner would proceed just as if nothing had happened. Oddly, no one would address it, almost as if to do so would anger her. It was an exceptionally weird and scary time and we labored under just as exceptional and scary circumstances. We knew that dramatic changes had taken place in my mother, but were helpless regarding how to respond to them or fix them. We were aware of a type of double loss. The first and worst being the loss of my father's presence, and the second being my mother's absence. We were powerless and after all, only children. But somehow each of us knew in some dark recess of our young mind that somehow we would have to grow up quickly, and God willing, we would do it and survive whatever else life would bring us, Because in all likelihood, my mother would be unprepared to do so.

CHAPTER FIVE

My mother. I have already addressed some of the trauma she experienced following my father's loss. I don't think it's necessary to detail all the early events of her life. Suffice it to say that she had been raised under relatively difficult circumstances. Her mother had died when she was still a child. Her father was a native of Ireland, who had emigrated when the prospects of life in Ireland appeared bleak. He had married a young Irish girl and joined the New York City Fire department as had thousands of young immigrants of his generation. Children arrived quickly, and the young couple soon had two daughters and two sons. Before the youngest boy was out of infancy, my grandmother developed breast cancer. She died at home when the oldest child was only ten years old. My grandfather came from the school of "no nonsense" and he was totally unprepared to be the single parent of four small children. Left with these little ones to raise, he apparently never found the delicate balance between discipline and love. He had too much of the first and too much inhibition to show any of the second. So for my mother life couldn't have been easy. Like most young girls of her time, after high school she went to work in the city. She continued to live in her father's house and like her other siblings, was required to contribute her paycheck, minus the money he would give her for expenses. Saturday night was the one night that she was allowed to go out, and at a girlfriend's party she met my father. She was twenty-three, and he twenty-one, and although she was engaged to someone that she had grown up with, she fell in love quickly with the handsome boy with the lightning wit. As she told the story, it took some doing, but eventually she prevailed and they married.

It was difficult for them in the early years. Money problems, extended family interference and different viewpoints complicated a marriage that just may have happened too young. My father found it hard to give up his single life and would often be at the bar with his friends until late in the evening. Either that or he and his brothers would stay up through the night playing cards and my mother would return home alone. So they argued in the early years over all those things that beset a couple that experiences youth, money problems and children arriving all at the same time. If my mother disapproved of something, her way of communicating that was to verbalize her displeasure ad nauseum. Even that didn't change his behavior substantially in those early days, but it did keep the tension between them alive.

My mother could be tough despite her delicate appearance. At five feet zero she could lower the temperature in a room if she were provoked, which she often was. Her repetition of the perceived offense would give way to a stony silence, the duration of which was always undetermined. It could be brief or last for days.

To her children this was a fearful situation. We worried if her avoidance of us would be permanent and for a young child, that is a scary prospect indeed. I remember fearing her more than my father. It was probably a result of her being the one home all the time and my perception of her volatility. As much as I depended on her, I dreaded upsetting her. And it would be that way throughout our relationship.

Early on in the marriage and soon after his own father was killed in the Fire Department, for reasons unknown to the family, my father took the exam and joined the department himself. Perhaps it was because as the oldest boy, he felt obliged to continue the family legacy, or perhaps he didn't know what else to do as a career at that time in his life. Or more positively, maybe he was drawn to the job for the challenge that it represented. I never understood why and the answer was never given. The pay for firemen at that time was extremely low, and didn't lend itself to the support of a wife and children, so Dad decided to take another job with an engineering company as a draftsman. Added to that he entered St. John's Law School in the hopes of eventually earning his law degree and retiring into private practice from the Fire Department. His plan was to retire after twenty years of service, at the age of forty-one. He would be pensioned and supported as he started his practice and that was important to him. It was an incredibly ambitious schedule. One which kept him from home almost around the clock. I don't believe it was so much that he wanted to be away, as much as his need to do everything he thought he was capable of and not miss an opportunity. He was young, smart, and wanted to do it all. Like all of us, I guess he thought that he had the time…and at that time there was really no reason to believe differently.

So my mother did what all young women her age did through those years. She cared for us as well as she was able, kept house, and thought that she was supporting her husband in his responsibilities to be the breadwinner. Over the course of those years, she suffered three miscarriages and the death of her oldest child. She had given birth to a son who had survived only two weeks. She did the best she could with the finances but creative and frugal as she tried to be, it was often not enough. But she endured somehow, and so did he. Probably because to an Irish Catholic mother life offered no other options. And if it had, she would not have chosen them.

When my father was killed, my mother seemed to retreat into "survival" mode. She developed anxieties. She was often concerned about neighbors and family being duplicitous which was probably an extension of the fear she felt being alone with four young children. As I look back now through the eyes of experience as a mental health professional, I am persuaded to draw some conclusions.

I believe that she was always depressed, probably from childhood as so many individuals are, and that her depression deepened after my father died. As anxiety is often a companion of depression, I believe that she exhibited that symptom to a diagnosable degree. The problem was that in the nineteen fifties no one in her circle

45

of experience went to therapists. At least no one in the Bronx, unless they were certifiable. And that would have been a dark family secret that would not have been discussed.

The others, and there were many if we can compare to present usage of services, lived those quiet lives of desperation without help. Remember too, that there were no medications to address depression issues so they were not an available option to alleviate any of the symptoms that she exhibited.

Adding to her feeling of isolation, after the initial visits and solicitous phone calls, there were really no dependable male figures to offer her help. Although my father had four brothers who expressed their devastation at his loss, his family really did not contact us much following his death or remain in our lives.

I'm uncertain regarding whether that was due to their lack of interest, or my mother's failure to issue an invitation, but I tend to believe the former. Had any of them not felt comfortable with my mother or had past issues with her that were unresolved, there were certainly opportunities to contact us, his children.

Whatever the reason, their contact with us came in the form of Christmas cards and we knew that we would never be able to depend on them. Not for a concept of family, not for finances, and certainly not for comfort. She grew to resent his brothers and so did we. Or at least three of us did. They would became enmeshed in our perceptions of abandonment, and rightfully so. Years of rumination and speculation have not changed my personal perspective of my father's family. I always felt that they had absolutely no excuse for their disinterest, and I still do. In their absence we had to adjust to a double loss. His and his family. An awful task for young children. As I said, they had no excuse.

In their absence, they lost the opportunity to know anything about our lives, and we theirs.

But, back to my mother. In her dependency, she began to live vicariously through us and what we accomplished. Perhaps that was the reason why it was so important that we not fail, or even come in second at whatever we put our hands to. Coupled with her need not to have any more to deal with, this became a requirement if we were to have peace in the house.

We children learned that lesson well and it would be years until we would be able to allow ourselves not to have to excel at every undertaking, at all times. She would often invoke a very harmful litany that would serve to keep us bound to the yoke of performance. If any of us would do something wrong that drew the attention of "outsiders", my mother would usually point out the "consequence" of marring my father's memory. She would point out that we would be responsible for disparaging him by our behavior. Really, I think that she was trying to deter us from repeating bad behavior. But the burden of preserving his memory would be heavy indeed.

One would not have to have a graduate degree in Human Behavior to understand the damage that such a statement could inflict on a child but then again, in personal survival mode, it was the best that she could do in all probability. Certainly, it was not her intent to inflict damage; she just needed us not to add to her own sense of burden.

I don't want to paint a picture that is a poster for maternal dysfunction with my mother. Across the years, the cacophony of her rebukes, her unwitting pressures, or even her enmeshment with us; the memory of that comes with less intensity and I see a person who was driven by sadness, fear and inability. She was doing her best to finish the job of raising a family on her own. I understand the fear of having more "shoes drop" and the deep need to avoid more pain. I see a woman with very little finances on the verge of poverty, (There were no funds for us then) hoping to urge them to success so that they may be scholarship educated. And, at the end of the day, we were. Was it misguidance? Yes. Did we incorporate a skewed view of our selves and what was required of us? Certainly. Was it the best way, or even a desirable way to raise children? Absolutely not. But it was the best she had to offer and it would have to be filtered through our own sense of forgiveness and understanding.

She was herself a broken vessel. No doubt she carried much of that baggage into her marital home with her, but it could only be exaggerated by the circumstances that she had to contend with. Truly, I see her as a wounded child, dependent upon her equally wounded children to keep her afloat in an uncertain current. Her tolerance of difficulty was low, probably because of her inability to handle it. She required the best of us for reasons of her own, and that expectation would be a blessing and a curse long into our adulthood.

CHAPTER SIX

My sister Joan was the oldest of the four children. The night my father died, she was two months shy of her sixteenth birthday and a sophomore in a girl's Catholic high school in the Bronx. Joan was studious, unlike the rest of her siblings, and her study habits combined with native ability made her a wonderful student. She was minimally social having only a few friends, but like my father had a sharp wit and an ironic sense of humor. If anything she tried to stay "under the radar" allowing the other kids to take the forefront either through their good or bad behavior. Being the oldest, Joan was closest to my grandmother, Daddy's mother. She spent more time with her than anyone else, and even shared some of my grandmother's interest in sewing and domestic skills. She could listen for hours to my grandmother's lilting Irish brogue, as she would recall stories of her life in Ireland. That was far more than we others would do, finding other distractions more appealing than Nanny's reminiscences.

It was Easter vacation for her in April of 1956. Joan had been invited to visit one of my uncles in Maryland with my grandmother. Since this was a once in a lifetime invitation she could barely contain her excitement and superiority at having been selected to go. The night of the fire was the second night of her stay and she and my grandmother were called home following the identification of the men. Joan was completely devastated. She would later recall having little memory of the trip home. She remembered that it was raining.

She had favored my father between her parents and felt totally abandoned to a mother that she neither understood nor bonded with. She went through the motions of the three-day wake barely able to maintain her sanity. Somehow she made it past the funeral services. From that time on, she withdrew into herself and her studies. Anytime that she could legitimately be outside of the house, she was. Any activity that required after hour participation, she joined. When she was at home, she was either studying, or taking me to a department store with her to browse aimlessly.

Joan and I shared a bedroom, although our age difference was significant. She was a teen and I was a toddler, but the demand for space superceded comfort. I remember waking up during the night and looking over toward her bed, and hearing her cry. It was heartbreaking the way she would whisper "Daddy..." over and over. It was as if she was begging him to answer. Even at the age of three, I knew not to interrupt her on these nights. It seemed to me that disturbing her would have caused her shame at having been discovered. I don't know how but I knew this inherently. The thing I suspect, after all these years is that she felt utterly alone and undefended. Withdrawal would become her method of survival and her personality was more compatible to the role of the "Lost child" that is so typical in hurting families.

In deference to my mother's volatility, she tried hard to draw no fire. If it would help her get by, she would keep a low profile. It did and she did.

I think that she believed that the only way to survive was to bury her pain in some work that would be both distracting and worthwhile.

And she took on that agenda seriously. But in the years following this, Joan became the scapegoat of the other siblings teasing and misbegotten humor.

Because she was removed from the mainstream of the sarcastic humor that passed for family interaction, and not particularly favored by my mother (for reasons unknown to us) she was perceived as fair game. No holds were barred when it came to harassing her. She was a perfect foil in that she would rant and rave in frustration, while the brothers and I enjoyed her reaction immensely. She was often the focus of many of the practical jokes or name calling that we would bandy about, the patsy of every practical joke, and the "sissy" who would go out of her way to get her brothers and sister in trouble with my mother. She would seemingly just wait to inform on one of us and of course, that rationalized the other kid's treatment of her. We used to say that she must have been the true result of some relationship that my mother must have had with a milkman, but my brother would say that no "self respecting" milkman could be pinned with that, and we'd laugh ourselves senseless. Truth be told, some of the things that she suffered and jibes she had to endure are STILL funny, although much of the sarcasm and scapegoating was a method of releasing the anger in the rest of us and we had no other outlet for it.

It was so passive aggressive in retrospect. Teasing her to the point of her explosion so that we could feel the release of that very anger we couldn't admit in ourselves. It became a family tradition in time, and one that should never have been allowed to perpetuate, much less be emulated. The more separation she felt, the further she would bury herself in her books or work. Unlike in other families, "book smarts" wasn't acknowledged in mine. It seemed that no one else had to study and since that became a source of pride to those of us that maintained excellent grades, that too became the focal point of many of the sibling jokes.

My brother used to say that we should call Joan "Bonzo" because he said that if Bonzo the Chimp studied as hard as she did, he would get good grades too. So true to form, the nickname "Bonzo" came into being and lasted for quite a while. As a result, even with her defense mechanism that she had adopted to bury her pain and abandonment, Joan couldn't be safe. A cycle developed that would be as self-sustaining as it was defeating. The more pain she felt, the more she would retreat into her books to attain some type of refuge. The more she retreated, the more she was ridiculed for her isolation. It was a no win for her and surely, equally a no win for her siblings who needed to be encouraged and allowed to express their own frustration in more honest and productive ways.

Joan continued to immerse herself in her studies and won an academic scholarship to the same university that my father had attended. Although she wanted to further follow in his footsteps and eventually attend law school, a health concern kept her from doing so. (She would later discover after years of restriction for a suspected heart problem that the diagnosis was in error.) She would contribute financially to the house, as would we all when and as soon as we could work, and then she came into a time when she would date. And she did so regularly. Her brothers may have found some physical features to berate, but in truth, she was a beautiful girl.

When she was twenty-three years old, she met the man who would become her husband. They worked together and from the description of him, we thought that he was the heir apparent to take over the company. In reality, he was a young man from the Bronx, twenty-six years old with an affected English accent and a nice car.

Of course, anyone who owned a car was considered prosperous to us, and he certainly looked the part with his ascot and cigars. What he also had was a mean and vicious temper which he showed quite often before the wedding, and even more after.

He was the classic abuser. Physical, emotional, verbal; and of course, she was crazy about him.

He was her first big love, in addition to being her ticket out of the house and those two elements kept her bound in an engagement and then a marriage for far too long. I remember a time a month after her marriage when she called our house crying hysterically. She said that her husband had struck her and my brothers both raced to her apartment to confront him. It truly boggles the mind to consider the ramifications of that, doesn't it? Her two tormentors, banned together to defend their sister against the outsider who took their places. But that was the way with us. We could do what we wanted; say what we pleased, and mistreat each other with abandon. An outsider however, could not. We would move heaven and earth to protect and rescue each other from that kind of trouble. Because she had warned him of their coming, her cowardly husband had thought better about being home and confronting two avenging angels. Wisely, he had disappeared somewhere. They made sure that she was as all right as she could be and then they came home. She unfortunately, did not. So went the relationship for the next eleven years and four children. When she finally did leave it was not for lack of love or even wanting to heal herself. It was because he had started to beat the children. I believe her attraction to this man had everything to do with the role she played within the family and those unresolved issues that resulted from my father's death. He could be the giver of gifts, which would certainly have been a distinct difference from her family life in which finances never allowed luxuries.

He was tall – six feet eight inches tall – and could portray a man who could be protective as well as "respected". Of course, that would be important to the child of a hero who had that as a guideline in her search for a mate that could compare to her father. Perhaps she envisioned a future that would have looked like the one she would have had had her father survived.

Her husband- to- be, with his physical size and strong presence, would be able to provide for her needs or so she reasoned. But he could be volatile which made him emotionally unavailable to her. What stronger (even if unconscious) connection could exist between her husband's unavailability and her own father's, which was so final? In the case of her fiancé though, he would return after his outbursts and that was the essential difference. It would not be as final. She would be able to experience someone going and COMING BACK...something had not happened before. And in that way the story of loss is allowed to have a different ending. After all, isn't that what survivors hope for? Last and certainly not least, this man represented an "out". He would be the deliverer. He would take care of her and legitimize the need to leave the home that she feared to leave on her own.

Psychological studies reveal consistent patterns. That we seek to repeat our painful experiences, and try to bring about a different ending.

It is the true definition of insanity – to keep repeating the same behavior and somehow thinking that the very next repetition will be different.

As individuals, we want to finally be able to resolve our past by doing it over in the present. Not a bad objective really, but unfortunately, we choose what has been familiar to us in our pasts.

In other words, we choose the same type of personalities and people and scenarios, often with the same issues that we wrestled with in the past, and attempt to mold it and change it to something that does not end badly for us. We want so much to believe that this time it will be different. It is a sad and noble quest for us to attempt to finally get the: love, relationship, understanding, etc. that was needed and still is needed. The problem is that we pick the same type of people and circumstances that we were originally injured by. We do this because while hoping for a different ending, we seek what's familiar. And what's familiar is the pain we experienced in former relationships. It's like the equation of one and one equaling two. The number "one" is familiar to us. We keep adding them. The problem is that we seek to get the hoped for "two"…the correct answer…but somehow, we always end up with "three".

What we have failed to realize is that we have not balanced the equation because we didn't know how. We were really adding "one" and "two", so "three" was totally predictable. But we did it over and over, hoping that the answer "three" would somehow be different.

Whatever the source of that pain, we will repeat it until we have dealt with it on our own. It is an immutable and certain fact as likely to happen as night following the day. In Joan's case, as in all of ours, she knew emotional abandonment (father's death) and mistreatment (family dynamics) and recreated these elements by entering into a relationship with an abusive person. He would act out his displeasure with her for some imagined infraction, and she would go through every hoop there was to regain his attention and esteem. She had experienced the ill treatment and the need to be rescued. When her husband would invariably act out she would experience both once again.

She held the belief that had my father lived she would not have been as put upon, but she chose someone abusive because that was what she was used to. The pining for a savior would be the drive but the reality would be what was familiar. It didn't change her desire to change the reality though, and she would try to make him love her enough to treat her well and be what she needed him to be.

The "Hero-ization" of my father (posthumous medals, recognition of sacrifice) could easily be transferred to this man that she could "look up to", if only he would change. It is the passion of any woman that has ever experienced some damage early. They are compelled to fix what was broken in their lives, and so fix themselves. Of course, in Joan's case (and much of my interpretation could be speculative) her husband's stature and his physical attributes may also have represented to her a parental presence.

It really doesn't fall that far out of the known predilection of persons from dysfunctional families to seek to finally have their needs met via their marital partner. When a child experiences trauma such as the sudden death of a parent, the balance in their world is forever compromised. Life becomes uncertain, unfriendly. There is usually a perception of a lack of security and safety, and that need may submerge and resurface later in life as the grown child seeks resolution of the early loss. The child of a hero is perhaps even more effected that others. Having to memorialize their parent, they may eventually seek to replace the "larger than life" persona in their significant relationships. I believe that my sister would have experienced this common reaction when she married the tall, charming abuser. Someone who, in the final analysis, would be hard to please, abusive and "absent."

Even as her father had been absent for those long years past. Even as her mother was hard to please.

Her husband had seemed able to rescue her from the dark and scary things of a child's world...like her Dad would have done had he had the opportunity.

The far-reaching effects of my father's loss for this oldest sibling began soon after she experienced the trauma.

The role that she assumed in the family of "lost child" was taken because the role that anyone assumes is always consistent with their individual personality. She found it easier to be introspective and studious, and she retreated into herself because she felt more comfortable there than in a frequently hurtful world. Her choices of careers, friends, and ultimately, a husband would be designed to compensate for the huge loss she had suffered. Just as with anyone, unless that enormous grief is dealt with over time, it still will drive our behavior. Joan was no exception. She wanted the family she had lost. But predictably, she found what she had known from an early age, more loss.

She raised the children on her own, got them counseling. Got herself counseling, but still kept the tendency to isolate that she had developed early on, together with the anxiety of unanticipated calamities that could possibly come her way. Interestingly, my mother was like that. You always had the idea that she just waited for the next calamity, and lived her life in that kind of anticipation.

Especially after my father died. Both she and Joan had been deeply traumatized by the suddenness of tragedy, and could never quite shake the anxiety associated with "what could happen."

Has Joan significantly recovered from some of the deepest injuries from both her past and her relationship? Possibly not. She still fears leaving home and her anticipatory stress takes different forms at different times. She fears receiving bad news, being old and alone, and sometimes being abandoned. She even worries despite her deep faith, that if she doesn't do everything exactly right in relation to God that He will withdraw from her. She knows intellectually that there is no real need for her to strive to be good enough for God, but then she learned a long time ago that people often distance themselves unless you meet their standards. She is often crisis driven. Perhaps she thinks that if she stays in crisis mode she'll be ready for the big one that is sure to come. The anxiety has changed forms many times but in essence, it still lingers. Will it ever be gone? I hope so, but probably not. But since she has sought to do a lot of personal healing work, it has become less powerful than it was in directing her emotions. And that is perhaps the best and the most that we can hope for. In the end though, for me it comes down to my being her sister. I lived her past with her, I watched her in those nights that she thought no one could see her pain when I was but three years old, and I came to understand. And…that makes all the difference.

Mom and Dad right after their marriage.

My mother holding newborn baby John. Behind her (left) my grandmother and at right my father's cousin Frances.

John, Brian, and I the Christmas before my father died.

Fighting the deadly fire: Hoolan and Hanson (#4 and #5)

ED CARROLL ASSESSING THE WALL
MOMENTS BEFORE HE RAN IN TO
WARN OTHER FIREFIGHTERS.

The aftermath: Six men lost in collapse of the wall.

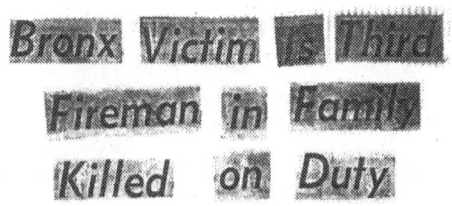

Firemen Who Died in Bronx Blaze

EDWARD J. CARROLL
Engine Company 48

CHARLES J. INFOSINO
Headquarters

ARTHUR G. HANSON
Ladder Company 44

FRED. J. HELLAUER
Engine Company 48

JOHN J. MALLOY
Engine Company 48

WILLIAM F. HOOLAN
Ladder Company

This clipping came from John's scrapbook.
It features pictures of the six men who died
at the fire.

6 Firemen Die In Collapse Of Bronx Factory

Six firemen were killed and six others were injured Wednesday night when they were caught in the collapse of a blazing Bronx building which nearly trapped Fire Commissioner Edward F. Cavanagh, Jr., and Deputy Commissioner George F. Land.

Some 75 firemen, with 100 policemen helping, were battling the five-alarm fire in a one-story structure at 4065 Third Ave., between 174th and 175th Sts., when the disaster struck.

WEAKENED by the flames, the front wall of the burning building was dragged down in a heap by a badly marquee. Several of the victims were atop the building and were plunged down into the flaming rubble. Others were caught directly under the tons of debris.

The building had been used recently in the manufacture of artificial flowers.

On orders of Commissioner Cavanagh, names of the dead were withheld until it was certain the families had been notified officially.

However, police identified the dead as:
Lt. John Malloy, Engine 48.
Edward Carroll, Engine 48.
Arthur Hassett, Hook & Ladder 44.
William Roulan, Hook and Ladder 44.
Charles Infosino, Engine 33.
Fred Hellman, Engine 48.

THE INJURED, all of whom were reported in fair condition at

Continued on Page 30.

6 Firemen Die In Bronx Blaze

Continued from Page 2

Morrisania Hospital, were identified as Assistant Fire Chief Antonio Petronelli, who suffered a broken leg; James Ogden of Engine 94, Joseph O'Keefe of Engine 41, Harold Hennie and Albert Choete, both of Engine 48 and Edward Cerrone, 40, of 1367 Purdy St., Bronx.

O'Keefe, a fireman three years, said at the hospital where he had four and knee injuries:

"I WAS on a ladder leaning against the outside of the building, trying to chop a hole in the roof. My buddies were on the roof, putting a hole in the bottom of the wall for the hose stream—to get ventilation," said streak.

"Got out just in time.

"Before I could climb to the whole front wall started—there was a weird cracking sound all around me. The men underneath didn't have a chance. I was lucky. I was thrown clear and rolled with the fall."

Shortly after the wall collapsed, a disaster unit arrived from Bellevue Hospital with a dozen doctors and several nurses.

The blaze, of undetermined origin, broke out shortly after 8 p.m. and raged with such fury that five alarms had been turned in by 8:45, when the wall caved in.

Officials speculated that chemicals in the making of artificial flowers fed the flames and seemed to resist the tons of water poured into the building.

More headlines. The smaller clipping references my father's call to his fellow firemen to run.

The article that featured my grandmother's many losses. She lost her husband, brother in law, and son in the line of duty for the FDNY.

Five caskets are carried into St. Patrick's Cathedral in Manhattan.

IRROR, TUESDAY, APRIL 10, 1956

Heroes' Rites for Firemen
6,000 March in Cortege on 5th Ave.
By HARRY ALTSHULER

New York bowed its head in grief Monday as six firemen who lost their lives in the collapse of a blazing Bronx factory building last Wednesday were laid to rest. Cardinal Spellman celebrated a Pontifical Solemn Requiem Mass in St. Patrick's Cathedral for five of the men.

A SLOW - PACED, heavy - hearted procession accompanied the bodies to the cathedral, in a spontaneous exhibition of sorrow and sympathy that mushroomed far beyond expectations. The dead men's relatives, high public officials, and more than 6,000 uniformed firemen took part in the cortege down Fifth Ave., while from the sidewalks crowds of up to 50,000 paused in silent tribute.

The mass death of six men was the worst disaster suffered by the department since 1932, when eight firemen lost their lives in the Ritz Tower explosion.

The procession started from 59th St., moving south to the cathedral at 51st, led by a mounted police detail and the Fire Department band. Fire Department engine pumpers were converted into caissons to carry the caskets. Behind the band, which played Chopin's Funeral March and other dirges walked Mayor Wagner, Fire Commissioner Cavanagh, Bronx Borough President James J. Lyons, Manhattan Borough President Hulan Jack and City Council President Abe Stark. They were followed by firemen, 16 abreast.

THEN CAME THE caissons, and behind them, 60 limousines bearing the widows and children of the dead men.

As the cortege passed St. Thomas Protestant Episcopal Church at 53d St., the church bells were tolled, and at the cathedral the bells of the pumping engines were sounded.

The caskets were brought into the cathedral according to rank and seniority of the deceased: first that of Lt. John P. Molloy, then those of Firemen William F. Roolan, Edward J. Carroll, Charles J. Infosino, and Frederick J. Reissner.

The mourners were escorted to special pews by firemen serving as ushers. Most were in tears as the bodies were carried inside.

Also attending the services were students of the senior class at Ursuline Academy, a Catholic girls school attended by Fireman Roolan's daughters, Joan and Maryanne; and a group of boy students from Our Lady of Mercy parochial school where Fireman Carroll's son is a student.

AFTER THE CATHEDRAL services, the caissons carried the caskets to the quarters of Engine Co. 65 at 33 W. 43d St., its entrance draped in black and purple as 80 firemen stood at attention. Taps were sounded, three volleys fired by a department rifle squad, and the muffled bell of the company's truck was tolled.

All the firemen in the procession appeared voluntarily, it was pointed out. About 2,500 were expected, but 5,000 appeared, and the number was...

Article from the New York Daily Mirror.

April 9, 1956. My mother enters St. Patrick's Cathedral for the funeral service for five of the six men. Brain is on her left and one of my uncles escorts her. John walks with his head lowered behind them.

An illustration from the New York Times.

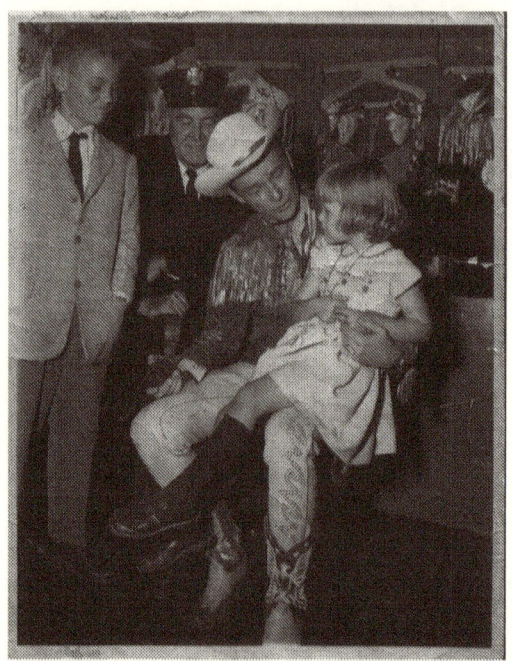

Brian and I posed for an FDNY publicity photo with Roy Rogers in May, 1958. Gerry Ryan head of the UFA in background.

CHAPTER SEVEN

On April 4, 1956, my oldest brother John was thirteen years old and in the eighth grade of a parochial school in the Bronx. He was an exceptionally smart and well-liked kid, given a bit to the Irish introspection, but only enough to make him interesting rather than maudlin. He was due to graduate grammar school in June and had already received a scholarship to Regis High School. Regis was a secondary school known for its academically superior student body as well as its rigorous discipline of its young scholars by the Jesuit priests that operated it. It was a prestigious thing to be accepted and John had run all the way to the firehouse the day he had received the news that he had been admitted. He wanted my father to be proud of him, to notice him. John felt sorely the frequent absences of my father and needed to draw the attention of this man that seemed to have such a big interest in things outside the home that it took almost all of his time. He needn't have run, though. I'm told that my father didn't seem to be excited about Regis, but reacted by saying, "Come back when it's a college scholarship." John would later recall his disappointment in that answer and would spend countless hours trying to decipher what my father meant. Speculation has spanned the years of course, and it is generally accepted that Dad's intent was to keep John focused, with his eye on the next objective. I don't know but I can only imagine how that off hand comment might have hurt a young boy who had only wanted to please.

When my father died, John spent hours putting together scrapbooks of newspapers that described the fire and the men that had fought it. He would meticulously cut out the articles, paste them into picture albums and illustrate them in his own hand, using his impressive artistic ability. He would pore over the books as if by piecing them together, he could somehow put his own world back together again. John got quieter, but stepped into the role that was being thrust upon him, and metamorphasized into a thirteen-year-old co-parent to the family and surrogate spouse to my mother. It was John's arm that she would clutch when she began her nightly choking episodes at dinner. It was his face that would go white as he made sure that she was all right, and satisfied himself that he wasn't going to lose another parent so soon after his father. It was John who, at the tender stage of pre-adolescence, was given a responsibility that should never have been foisted upon a child who had just suffered a loss of such magnitude. But he put his head up and he did it. I think now that he didn't believe for a moment that he had a choice and truthfully, he was probably right.

In the roles taken by children in dysfunctional families, John would have been the "hero". He excelled at school, he had close friends, he was kind and smart, and he was so well thought of inside the family and without, that he could command respect from the other siblings. I remember saying to my sister when I was older that John was born wearing a fedora, and it seemed so true that we wouldn't even laugh. He took his place as head of the household with aplomb and things actually had a type of stride until he hit his first wall. Curiously it did not happen as expected in the early days after my father's death. If was about eight months later, and during his first year at Regis that his world collapsed again.

Having taken offense at the way a teacher had treated a friend of his, he locked himself away in his bedroom and refused to go to school, to talk, to eat, or to function. It was as if there had been a crack in his armor that had festered over months and no one had noticed, until it all hit the ground around him with a sickening thud. In retrospect, I believe that the defense mechanism that protected him from the enormity of my father's death in the immediate aftermath started to shatter. I believe that his grief and anger (transferred to the priest who had hurt his friend) had risen up to engulf him. For days he isolated himself and for days my mother pleaded with him until unsure of what else to do, she had one of the priests he had bonded with at Regis come to the apartment to speak with him.

When that was done, the man emerged from John's room to announce that John did not want to return to Regis, but wanted and needed to attend another school. He told my mother that he was willing to attend the public high school, but since that was not the safest environment for an Irish Catholic boy even then, she insisted on sending him to another, less known boys parochial school. It was from here that he graduated. Isn't it odd that he felt compelled to leave the school that had the market on excellence and achievement? Is it not equally odd that it was the object of one of the last conversations he had had with my father, and that my father had not acted impressed with his success? I can speculate all kinds of motives on John's part, but really, accept to signal a decompensation into grief, this issue and its reasons remain vague, and took a back seat to his later life choices. Interestingly, as an adult he would always regret his transferring to the other school. And typically, he never saw it within the context of an emotional necessity at that time but only that it was something that he had achieved that he had failed to complete. Even so, John seemed to put himself back together after leaving Regis. He went to and completed high school with honors, oversaw the care and discipline of his other siblings, continued in the parent-surrogate spouse role, and kept his unique social leadership among his peers. Like all of us would when we were able, he worked at some job from the time someone would hire him, which was usually long before he got his official working papers. Like my sister before him, he contributed to the household most of what he earned. Then it was college where he worked hard, continued to date his high school girlfriend, kept his job and sustained his management of the family responsibilities.

John was the son everyone wanted, the friend that you never wanted to lose touch with. He was the soul of wit, and the master of brevity. He got things done, he saw things through, was the top of the class, the leader of the pack, and the star of the neighborhood. In reality he was driven to excel, and maybe finally to match accomplishments with his hero father. John never spoke much about him. Except for the occasional story, he held his feelings about my father's death as well as most personal matters very close to the vest. No one really noticed it because they were grateful to have the replacement for my father and help for my mother. They needed him to be what he was, and if it was detrimental to him they didn't notice it because they didn't want to. He was incredibly and competently busy, and it took up his life, spare time, and energy. John wanted to become a lawyer. He had his father's Law Dictionary as well as other texts that he had used while he attended St. John's Law School. Perhaps the role of being the replacement that he had inherited also lent itself to completing his father's career path and practicing law as his father had not had time to do. John entered law school determined to succeed. My brother, ever the multi-tasker, then married his high school sweetheart and worked full time for an insurance company during the day while he attended night classes. I forget exactly how many points those issues are worth individually on the Stress Scale, but suffice it to say that individually they rate fairly high. But we were quite used to personal stress and performance and achievement in my household, so possibly he felt little difference save directing his energies in new areas. John was golden. We all expected him to shine and he did not disappoint us. He graduated from law school second in his class, although he was the only one among his classmates that held a full time job while going to classes. Of course he was disappointed that he was not first, but gamely befriended the fellow that was. They would remain close for many years. He had a daughter by this time and was just at the point of starting his career in his own newly formed company in Manhattan.

His star was rising and we were proud of his achievements and the fact that he had overcome so much adversity - the death of my father, all of the responsibility he had taken, financial hardship, and the myriad of other things that made his life harder than most of his friends. Through him we all succeeded, even if vicariously. His triumphs were ours and we used him as a role model to motivate ourselves to accomplishment. He had made it out of poverty and our apartment, the neighborhood and the past, and the probable future of more of the same for our generation and us. My mother favored him for these reasons and why not? He had reflected well on her efforts.

Three years into his career, his daughter became suddenly and seriously ill. A miscalculation on the part of the hospital caused her to sustain brain damage. Five years following this, she passed away at the age of seven. I had not witnessed his immediate reaction to the death of my father, but I can say with certainty that his reaction to this loss was heartbreaking to see. He was devastated. Although she had lived the last five years of her life in a fairly vegetative state, her death came as a shock to him and he blamed himself. The autopsy revealed that she had died early in the morning and he felt that had he been awake, he could perhaps have resuscitated her from the cardiac arrest that took her life. It was an improbable thought but he held to it. He was somehow responsible. As he had always been. As he always would be.

John effectively collapsed during this time. We worried and waited.

It took over a year for him to regain his bearings. When he came back emotionally from this he was unable to speak of his child, and rarely would. He threw himself deeper and more frantically into work. It was the remedy he had discovered as a teenager. It was almost as if this loss had melded with the one of my father, and to survive he had to rely on what had worked before. The company thrived far beyond anything he and his partner could have imagined. He was comfortable financially, the mover of the business, father to two more girls, the titular head of the family of origin, and the dear friend of many. Somehow though, he remained driven. He seemed to be fueled by anger at times and we siblings would often shy away from his stinging comments. He was a dichotomy of sensitivity and harshness - the ying and yang of human emotion. The problem was, you never were quite sure what you were going to get. What he said pretty much went and it would be unwise to contradict him, lest you find yourself the target of immediate verbal incineration. He would tell you what he thought, but never what he felt. He would tell you what you were doing wrong, but often overlook the things you did that were right. I thought he was difficult and truthfully, for the most part I avoided him. I loved him but feared the criticism. He remained that way, I'd say, for most of his adult life, and it is only recently that he has mellowed, and appears kinder. The intense drive has gone and he has allowed himself to return to the kid he was, I think, before life happened to him. I like him now too, where I only loved him before. This change has happened because he is sick. It is not an act of will, or a result of special insight. It is not the change that occurs in a man once he has found God. It is because the nature of his illness causes one to process things differently. If not for that, it is possible that he may have lived his life driving the chariot fiercely, never noticing the people along the road he traveled. Or the fact that often he would hurt their feelings.

John's present condition makes me incredibly sad despite the positive changes it has brought about for him. I weep for the child that he was that never got a chance to be one. I weep for the weight upon thin little shoulders and his resignation and purpose as he took it on. He was so caught up in his need to perform and chase his father's memory that he could never rest, never relax. He could never permit himself to ease up because he was desperate for the approval that would never come. It is wrenching to think about a boy frozen in grief that used the anger of that to fuel his accomplishments but didn't know how to release it enough in his relationships. Not with the original family with whom he shared that loss. Perhaps he feared that closeness would compromise his role, or even that it would make him too vulnerable to perform that which he had to do. Or perhaps he just tucked everything inside to inspect at some later date that never seemed to come.

It is sad to think of a boy who sat in a room putting together scrapbooks of his father who felt the need to measure up to not only his expectations but everyone else's as well. He would have huge shoes to fill if he were to substitute for a hero. More than that, he would have equally huge shoes to fill just to be "good enough". And now that Dad was gone who knew when that was accomplished? The point is that it would never be defined but John would be forever driven to attain the impossibility of it.

In families that are dysfunctional, be it from the absence of a parent, deprivation of emotional or psychological nurturing or some other issue, the member that is capable of achievement usually assumes the role of hero. They have chosen a row that is hard to hoe, insofar as perfection is not easily attained, and the perception of the family by others is critical to it. All kinds of things may be going on behind closed doors but the hero maintains the public face of the family, and so accomplishes a presentation of normalcy and success. The hero is the rescuer, the star, the leader and role model. And John was no exception. He made my mother and indirectly, my father "look good". And we all not only let him, we encouraged him to do so. We needed it. We probably needed some hope for ourselves. But he took on that role and the old warning regarding becoming what you pretend to be was proven right. He became everything and more that the thirteen-year-old boy had to pretend to be. And he did it with such amazing skill that no one noticed the pain beneath the accomplishments. No one noticed his shoulders sagging under the responsibility.

I don't know if that would have changed had his illness not precipitated it. Most heroes maintain that role throughout their lifetimes because to surrender it would be to lose the identity they worked so hard to forge. Although I am dismayed at his condition, I am glad that he finally got to experience the permission to put down his load. He finally feels the freedom to do so without the usual guilt. It scares me to my bones, this illness. But even so, I have to celebrate his opportunity, whatever its source, to experience life free from the need to perform. Like I said, he's nicer. More than that we all get the chance to see the kid that hid behind his eyes for all those years even as he took the role of an adult. The child who he really was after all was said and done. The child who he was before a night in April made him grow up too quickly.

CHAPTER EIGHT

DAD: "How many times have I told you to come home on time?"

BRIAN: (Said plaintively.)"A million times, Dad. A million times".

DAD: (Taking off his belt by the sounds of it to us who sat in the next Room)"What do I have to **DO** to get you to listen?"

BRIAN: "I don't know, Dad. Maybe nothin."

Naturally, by this time the rest of us sat still as stones around the dining room table trying not to smile. Forks were held mid-air as we strained to hear. We were cringing at this point but didn't want to miss a thing. But as if by some miracle of timing, my father would suddenly realize that if he didn't leave right away he would be late for work. And he would have to "postpone" the beating until another time. It was always that way. Never failed. We would all look at each other every time, too. As if to say simply by the law of averages, one of these times Brian would surely get it. He never did, though. Good for him.

Brian. The third child down the line.

Born to be wild, smart, hilariously funny, and only eight years old when his father died. Brian was the brother closer in age to me and as a result, we always interacted more with each other than we did with the older two siblings. At the age of eight, he was a second grader in the same school as John. Like his older brother, he had many interests. His however, ran more to things such as: being late for dinner, running around the neighborhood like a wild man and tormenting his sisters. If someone told me that he was also smoking back then I probably would have believed him. Although I think that came later. Like when he was eleven.

Before my father's death, I remember them engaging in rituals like the one I mentioned that was called "Late for Dinner". No matter how many times he got in trouble on the few occasions that my father was home, Brian would walk in about halfway through the meal. He would come flying through the house with some excuse and run right into my father's frown. Every time. It got so routine that we would make bets on it. The one who picked closest to the time that Brian would actually show up would win. We still do it after all these years. Mostly, I win. I knew him better. But so his relationship with my father would go. Dad the disciplinarian. Brian the irrepressible wild card.

I really don't remember anything else about their relationship and I don't think it's because of my age because I remember too many other things vividly. Sadly, I think there is a possibility that that was the sum total of their interactions. And that would be the foundation of Brian's later story.

Then April 4th happened. Brian was allowed to attend the memorial services on April ninth, but right after they were over he and I would be sent off to the homes of relatives. The first uncle we went to was rather strict and Brian didn't do too well with that. He convinced my cousin to climb a tree in the early dawn hours to see into the neighbor's bedrooms. Needless to say, the neighbors were not amused when they saw two little kids watching their morning wakeup rituals. He would laugh when I was "fresh" to my aunt and of course, that would encourage me to keep going. Following little episodes like that he went home. I went to another uncle and aunt for the next few weeks. I believe that nothing out of the ordinary happened after that as everyone struggled to adjust to the changes. Until, that is, we went to a family christening later that year.

It was a party for the child of my father's brother. All the gifts and cards were piled on the dining room table. Later in the day, it was discovered that money from one of the cards was missing. The adults spent the day searching until eventually, Brian admitted to taking the money. He had pulled it from the card and flushed it down the toilet. My mother was horrified, shamed in front of the in-laws. The look that she passed Brian would have withered steel. We left under some type of a cloud that day and rarely were invited to any of the Carroll functions after. Brian was punished and his behavior was forgotten eventually. What was confounding was that no one ever questioned what motivated him. No one explored his feelings or even sought to discover why a little boy would do such a thing, and at a family event. What was he trying to express? Why would he pick that time and place? His behavior was addressed, certainly, and that is where it ended. Of course, it was not considered a remedy of the times to seek outside help. It was not even considered, much less acted upon. The stigma was great and a lower income parent with no background would not have professional counseling in their frame of reference. The true victim became the perpetrator, sentence was imposed and carried out, and life went on.

In 1958, two years after the christening incident, Brian became seriously ill. After weeks of failed ministrations by my mother, rheumatic fever had progressed so thoroughly that he became partially paralyzed before he finally was taken to a hospital. The illness had effected his spinal column and he was unable to even lift his head for a sip of water. The Fire Emergency squad had taken him in the ambulance and one of the medics later told my mother how close to death he had been.

Brian still tells the story of being delirious and "seeing" my father during that time. He said that the first night of his stay, Dad opened the door to his room, came in and smiled at him. Pausing only moments, he then turned, waved and walked out the door and down the hospital corridor. Brian said he had thought he would die, but knew he wouldn't when my father left the room without him.

All these years have passed, and he has never vacillated or changed his story. Maybe he wanted it so badly that what he experienced was a manifestation of his need, I can't say. But, I leave him to his story...

Brian took months to recover but when he returned to school he was able to resume his studies in the same grade that he was in prior to his illness. He was a smart kid, if not totally stimulated by the "rigors" of grammar school. For years he took penicillin daily which is how they treated residual heart murmurs back then. You might have thought that would have slowed him down a bit, but you would have thought wrong. Not him. He never lost his enthusiasm for a good street fight, pulling a practical joke, or ditching school for a corner poker game. He lived on the edge and was the essence of "cool". Smoking and drinking and playing cards were the after school sports he enjoyed most and true to form, he discovered these activities at the wizened age of eleven.

By the time he was in his teens, Brian was the one that my girlfriends swooned over. He was handsome, cocky, tough and smart. He was fearless. There was nothing that he wouldn't try, and often trouble would be attached to it. My mother would be beside herself trying either to keep up with his latest infraction or anticipate the next. He was the rebel. He fancied himself a young James Dean who reveled in his independence and took pride in being able to pull things off that most others wouldn't even attempt. He was funny, too. He'd make you laugh in spite of yourself even as he was smooth talking his way into your good graces…and your paltry savings…again.

And he had a special ability to make you regret being so exasperated with him only moments before…Unlike the rest of us, he never held an after school job for long. Invariably, he would decide not to show up and be terminated. What we didn't know then was that he would often be hanging out with his friends and drinking, a habit that he would nurture into addiction.

On those times that he did get himself into trouble, my mother would call in reinforcement in the person of John. As acting head of household, John would be charged with the task of applying pressure to Brian to get him back into line. Sometimes that pressure would look like trying to verbally reason with him and at other times, it might take physical coercion. Either way, it helped to forge a wedge between them. For all practical purposes, Brian resented the intervention of his older brother. Predictably. The relationship between them would be one of filial competition, comparison and inappropriate discipline and would grow increasingly strained. They were brothers but they always seemed to be on a collision course.

When Brian reached college age, he was admitted to Fordham University, the alma mater of his older siblings. He began his freshman year and seemed to struggle with the confines of his life and surroundings.

Not long into the semester he announced that he was going to California to do what most of the young people were doing at that time. He would go to the West Coast and "find himself". What an odd concept that was. The presumption was that personal identity and direction would be found simply by heading west until you reached the ocean...

He left in 1966, and would stay three years. We heard from him once a week in those days and I suppose we felt that he was doing okay. The specifics of his life and any information he offered about it were always vague. My mother didn't seem to prod him for information, either. During those times we concluded that no news was good news and left it at that. Where Brian was concerned, as long as he was avoiding any catastrophic problems, was neither incarcerated nor living on the street, we were thankful. John got together with him once while he was on a business trip to San Francisco. They memorialized the meeting with a picture taken at a bar. Evidently, Brian was still drinking.

Three years after his surprise departure he returned home just as abruptly. It is fair to say that it seemed as if his "self" still eluded him, as he was still searching and still acting uneasy in his skin.

The anger that had fueled so much of his earlier youth would still flare and had a new edge to it. It would boil to the surface in unpredictable ways whenever he was drinking. And he drank. A lot. The first few drinks would elicit a type of euphoria. He would be incredibly funny, talkative and the life of the party. But somewhere after the first couple and without any forewarning, he would turn mean. He would take offense at some imagined criticism and become scary. Threatening and dangerous, he would seek out situations that put him at risk. Whether it was provoking a fight with a stranger or a family member, he would literally be out of control. My older brother said once that he thought that Brian was unconsciously trying to provoke someone to kill him. He said that it was like a death wish that he had, depression rocketing to the surface driven by alcohol. I think that he was more right than he knew. I feared Brian a lot in those days. I was a teenager by then and knew the signs to watch for. When incited, his jaw muscle would twitch; a visible forerunner of the internal rage that was poised to erupt. Predictably, there would be some frightening episode to follow. There always was. But I also felt so sorry for him. I saw him as a kid that had been lost in the shuffle and never reclaimed. I thought I could almost see the despair hidden beneath the anger.

Despite the volatility, he met and married a young New York girl who had worked as his secretary at his job.

She lived through the erratic behavior, the disappearances and the nightmarish life of alcoholism. Naturally, she had experience with such chaos. Her background held alcoholics as well. Even with the birth of a daughter, Brian's behavior continued. He maintained employment despite nightly imbibing, and would begin drinking as soon as he reached home in the evening. He was spiraling into his addiction. Although he was able to keep his professional standing and engaging personality for the most part, his family was frightened for him.

Brian's relationship with them was erratic. With my mother he would be protective yet inconsistent. He would jump on anyone who would say something negative about her, and yet treat her shabbily himself at times. With John he maintained a distance, as he did with Joan, yet there were times that he went far beyond the ordinary to show them caring and kindness. With me he kept a closeness of sorts that would evolve into frequent visits and phone calls, but I never knew when one of those late night calls would be one in which he was drunk and provoking a confrontation. I learned to be wary of the traps he would set. He wanted you to respond a certain way so that he could launch into an angry tirade. I learned how to hang up on him.

We loved him, would be horrified by him, would rescue him, and would be angry with him.

After some debacle, I would always promise to break contact with him but would invariably relent. My mother did the same. She would be hurt and angry with him for some issue and before you knew it, she would be brushing it under the carpet and returning to business as usual. I think my mother always remembered how very ill he had been and how frightened she had been about losing him. And so she would forgive him everything. Much to our amazement she would ignore what was, while hoping for some miracle to come along to straighten him out and bring what could be. He was long past the stage that she could call in John to coerce him into line and because of that, she was left to her worry. Naturally, she never spoke to him openly about his drinking or any of his transgressions. In a dysfunctional family the elephants in the living room are ignored and the secrets are kept. Even among the members. She just added him to her list of anxieties and would do so until her death. Occasionally, she would want to believe the grandiose stories that he concocted. He would tell her incredible stories of his great financial successes, his extravagant purchases that somehow never materialized. For a time she would buy into it. She would need to believe that he was on the road to recovery, if only to lessen her burden of worry. When the truth inevitably was learned she wouldn't comment on the bizarreness but would seem to dismiss it. It was if she was waiting for the sequel so she could repeat the pattern and believe again. In that way I'm sure she handled that segment of her anxieties. To keep her fear in control she would have to compartmentalize and so, minimized the current stresses that she felt. And she felt many.

Quite a few years would pass with the status quo still in place. In 1982 Brian had a son, moved to the South Pacific for a position with a foreign government, and left home for yet another time. During his tenure there his alcoholism reportedly reached its peak. He experienced a few serious auto wrecks we later found out, but miraculously escaped without injury. He family life was in shambles. After three years on the island and on a trip to the States which was only to last for a few weeks, he returned to visit and John and I admitted him to a rehab facility. He was angry and unmoved by the intervention that we did but entered the facility anyway. I suppose that deep down he knew how bad off he had become. Thankfully, it "took", probably saving his life, and bringing him back to live permanently on the East Coast. It was the rock bottom that he needed to hit and although it took a while, he was back to the person he was and could have been before he picked up a glass and a fist to cover his pain.

Research indicates that by the age of seven a child in a dysfunctional home will decide upon a means by which they will escape some of the feelings that they have and want to alleviate. They will look around their world, at the adults surrounding them, and determine which one seems to be able to accomplish "good feelings". They will watch and ascertain by what methods these adults attain this and on some subconscious level make a decision to do the same. Brian was not unusual in his emulation of my father's trips to the tavern. What added to his emotional turmoil was a loss of that father who could have made the difference in his young life, and maybe seen the trouble that he was coming into at an earlier date. What made his loss even harder to bear was the absence of anyone that showed him love rather than discipline, and accountability rather than passivity.

He was effectively wearing his sadness and anger on his sleeve as a child of eight, when he made a bid for some – any kind of- attention at that christening party so many years before. His rebellious actions throughout the years was a walking testimony to the anger of grief, a need to be recognized as distinct from his older brother, and a deep and abiding need to identify with a father that he barely knew. Perhaps he gave up early on as being the second "hero" of the family. That place was already appropriated to John and he was too hard an act to follow.

Perhaps too, he felt that he could never live up to his father's legacy, and took every means he knew to prove it.

It must have been a further blow to realize that the parent who was remembered with only respect and pride was the one who was constantly angry at you, or at least, seemed to be. Brian's inability to remember anything but discipline from his father may have convinced him early on that he was the problem child. From that he could have concluded that he was not deserving of love. I can only imagine the pain of that to a young boy without the resources to ascertain if it were true. Especially after his father was gone. Or, perhaps all of those things. It seems that emotional motivations do not exist in a vacuum, and many different driving forces can exist in the same space. I only know with certainty that I felt pain for him. I felt pain for all of us.

But truly I still can't come up with an answer to something. Despite my age and experience, I cannot begin to understand why the needs of a child following such a stupendous loss were not recognized. I know better. As a therapist, I am certainly aware that these things happen all the time. Kids get lost in the immediate aftermath of a loss, and never resurface to any type of normalcy. But I continue to marvel at the dismissal of the trauma for a child that has been suddenly presented with the unanticipated loss of a father. It is incomprehensible to me that even the father's friends on the job overlook a little boy who has lost his father to heroism. Never mind the relatives. That people can disregard the children's needs and their tragedy is totally without redemption. That actions are not undertaken to help them heal from it – either from family or others that understand the danger of any service- is tantamount to criminal. It is an issue that cries out for change, and we must see to it. There is no wisdom in or excuse for compounding these kids' losses.

I know from personal experience that they can and do, though. They did with us.

CHAPTER NINE

The loss of my father when I was three years old would follow me throughout my life. In the earliest days following my comprehension that he would not be returning home again, I had nightmares. Although I don't remember them, I am told that I would wake up screaming every night for months, terrified that the ceiling of the apartment was falling in on us. I am also told that an uncle, trying to explain to a little girl why her father was gone, told me that my father had died when bricks fell on him. I suppose he thought that he was doing a good, if difficult, thing. I suppose he thought that it would be better if I knew some of the facts. He couldn't have been more wrong. I would have those dreams for years.

Early on I assumed the role of mascot probably because I could. I would use my verbal ability, humor, or any of the diversionary tactics I had learned to draw attention away from tension in the household. I would cajole my family members into laughing, and try to focus their attention away from any sadness or anger that they may have been feeling. And I did it well. As the youngest, I was home most often with my mother, and somehow assumed the arduous task of caretaking her emotionally. I could dissuade her from anger (at times) and keep her engaged. I became her sounding board at too early an age. I was precocious, and I was available, and I cared enough to assume the role. Everyone else seemed to be glad of it because it was one less responsibility my siblings would have to bear themselves.

I went through grammar school with highest honors. The expectation was unspoken, but very present.

I would not get praise for academic achievements; but certainly knew that if I did not perform, there would be my mother's extreme displeasure to face. She was intimidated, I think, by authority figures. Especially those that were in any type of religious orders, so to get in any type of trouble with them was to triple your chances of facing her wrath. I saw by brother Brian find that out on a regular basis and determined that I would avoid it at all costs. Luckily, I was smart and the teachers liked me, so at least that wasn't an issue. I knew very early on in my school career that I would have to get scholarships if I were to go to schools of my choice. I took on this task because I didn't want to burden my mother further, especially financially. I slipped further into my duties as her protector, and would continue to take the role quite seriously.

When I graduated from elementary school I had won six scholarships to local high schools. I had my pick with all tuition paid, but the pall over my graduation was that my mother was upset because the priest had not announced all of them from the stage. It disappointed me as well, but not so much that I wasn't pleased to finally be on my way to high school.

It was her issue but she was already dependent upon my successes to validate her own efforts at parenting. And perhaps too, she lived vicariously through the accomplishments of her children that she had not herself realized.

I aced high school, was popular enough to be elected president of the student body in my senior year. I was valedictorian and dated quite a bit, but usually one boy at a time. "Going steady" was the popular social situation of the time, and I usually was. Despite having a job from the age of thirteen, academics and activities filling my days, it seemed that my attentions lay foremost with boys and relationships. It is not that I was running around with them and being promiscuous. In that day, a girl who even thought about sex was in danger of losing respect from males as well as female peers. Besides that, I knew my mother would kill me if she ever got wind of my acting "loose". But really, I was already looking for a male replacement for the father that I had always missed.

I remember thinking about that one day while walking the ten city blocks to my job. I realized that day how much I missed even the everyday routine of having a father in the house. I wanted to be able to say something as simple as "I'll ask my father if I can go". I missed not being able to refer to a father like other kids did theirs. I would even have settled for a stepfather back then, but there had never been anyone in the picture. When I was nineteen, and working in downtown Manhattan, I would ride the bus and entertain myself during the ride with a fantasy. I would make believe that my father had not died, but that my parents had divorced, and since that was scandalous in the 1950's, they let everyone believe that he had died in that fire. I daydreamed that I would one day look out of the bus window and see him turning a corner. That I would find out where he lived and so find him and go to his house for an incredible and tearful reunion. It was a great fantasy, really, but one which would always cause me a deep sadness. I knew that even dabbling in that kind fantasy would make the reality that much harder.

Had I known then that I would be driven by the sheer loss to seek out the familiar…Had I known that I would seek to replace my father in the men that I would choose…I would have saved myself years of more tragedy.

I received an academic scholarship to a prestigious school in Pennsylvania, and although it meant leaving home and my mother alone since everyone else had left the house, I decided to go.

On some level, I made my decision based primarily on the knowledge that I had to loosen the ties between my mother and myself.

I had feared her dying all of my childhood and knew that in the day that would happen, I would have needed to have had time on my own being independent. It's not that she was sickly as much as she was at times a hypochondriac, and the anxiety I felt about her possible loss was overwhelming. I had already decided that I needed to expand my life for my own maturity, and maybe hers as well. Another factor was that I feared ending up in the Bronx for my entire life, marrying a local boy, and living with a family in one of the neighborhood apartments. I dreaded that. As scary as it was I had to strike out. Despite the outcry from mother, siblings and close friends, I packed my suitcase and left for school.

I found a totally foreign world seemingly filled with kids from privileged backgrounds, who were not on scholarship although very intelligent, and didn't really warm up right away to a kid from the Bronx. In spite of my dissimilar origins, I made fast friends with the girls on my dorm floor. I learned things from them, too. One thing was not to say I was from the "Bronx", but from "New York City". Apparently, the young scions of the wealthy families liked that better. I learned to dress, and I learned to be ashamed of my roots. I learned to miss the true camaraderie of my friends back home, even as I was fitting in to the upscale friendships of proximity rather than depth. I continued to look for the man of my father fantasies. He would be respected, protective, financially stable, handsome (preferably with the dark hair and blue eyes of the Irish) and of course, he would be emotionally unavailable. I would jump through hoops to perform for him, to earn his love, and in so doing, he would love me back and not leave or abandon me.

The blueprint was in place from the age of three but true to every dysfunctional script that exists, I was certain that this time it would be different. This time he would stay and love me. This time he would not die, choose a dangerous job over being with me, or disappear. I would make sure of it. The problem was, of course, that the only script that I had also provided me with the characteristics of the main player.

He WOULD be unavailable because that is what I knew. All I knew. He would not be attainable because what I also knew was how to perform for love. It was a recipe for relationship disaster but like the movie, it was my personal Ground Hog Day that I would replay over and over until the issue was resolved within me. It would really not be about the man I would choose, it was about me.

But before that resolution would ever occur, I would bash myself against many relationships with men that were an emotional equivalent of end stage dysfunction. I chose very successful men that were formidable, callous, incapable of bonding, but who liked the way I looked, and more importantly, how THEY looked when I was with them.

There was a lawyer who was incapable of personal attachment. There was a pastor who was totally unable to start a sentence that did not begin and end with him as the focal point. There was a man who claimed undying love and commitment and spent his days with other women. And as the coup d'etat: a physician that was as wealthy as Solomon, but who was verbally and physically abusive. And there was me. Totally convinced that I could change them. I would jump through whatever hoops there were whatever madness they offered. I would tolerate the intolerable and it nearly broke me. I was bankrupt physically, mentally and emotionally. I couldn't go forward, backward, around, or through. If I didn't deal with the loss, starting with the original one, I would never again be able to find my way out of the pain I was in. It was physical. It was visceral. And it was so old, this pain, that

115

it radiated through my chest like molten lead, weighing me down into depression.

It would be a long process. I would go through counseling, and examine the past. I would grieve, isolate, journal, talk and work hard to exhume the long buried feelings.

I would find God, commit my life to Him and with His help, walk through the process. Eventually I would become a therapist myself, specializing in Dysfunctional families and becoming a local catalyst for more recovery groups. I would spend ten years alone post divorce, unwilling to enter another serious relationship prior to resolving these personal issues. I would see my two children raised and in college, would work in my field, pursue knowledge of both God and man and do whatever it took to find healing.

For me the progress was slow but steady. It was a tough walk and I discovered that there is never an end to the journey. There are significant changes that are positive. Sometimes when I'm not vigilant, I have the possibility of slipping back into old patterns but mostly, I'm aware. I struggle with the concept of God as a Father, but that is normal considering the past. I sometimes struggle with making appropriate boundaries, especially with family, but I continue to work on it, realizing that our goal should be progress and that Perfection is only given to One.

And I met a man and married him. He is totally unlike anyone in my past in that he is kind, open and available. Had I not taken the time to delve into my own issues, I would have overlooked him in my quest to seek the familiar. But these days the familiar is different and it doesn't look anything like it used to. It used to be that all of my father loss issues got together in the same place and took the form of an emotional partner. It used to be that I would permit the unacceptable, determining to try harder to make a relationship work that should not have begun at all. In the past I would get hurt by treatment that was unkind or cruel, but hold it in for fear of risking someone else's displeasure. I don't know when that changed but I'm grateful that it did. These days if someone continually hurts my feelings I decide to avoid them rather than invite them into my life. Now don't get me wrong. There are people that have to be present in a peripheral way. But that's what I keep the relationship. Incidental and peripheral.

I don't think I'll ever get over the original loss of my father fully, though. That it no longer directs my choices will never dismiss the regret or sadness of having so vital a piece absent in the fabric of my life. I will never not miss my father; just as I will never not wonder how different life could have been had he stayed with us. I tend to want to surmise that things would have been better. Ask someone else who has survived a hero. I'll bet that they tell you the same thing.

CHAPTER TEN

Alcoholic parent(s). Workaholic parent(s). Absent parent(s). Emotionally distant parent(s). Emotional incest. Conditional love. Sudden trauma. Double messages. Mixed messages. Performance requirements. Using scapegoats in the family. Children as spousal replacements. Neglect. Excessive teasing. Fostering familial competition. "Martyrdom" of a parent. Uncertainty as to caretaking. Premature exposure to adult emotional issues or information. Inhibition, abandonment. Depression. Post traumatic stress of any family member.

Although the above list is certainly not an exhaustive list of characteristics, it does include many of the circumstances that can comprise the groundwork for a family to become dysfunctional. In families that have lost a parent, many of these issues undoubtedly apply just by the very nature of the loss itself. In families of heroes a number of dynamics that existed prior to the loss are overshadowed even if categorically dysfunctional, because of the very nature of the manner of death. In other words, if there were

119

issues in the family before, some of them will be minimized or denied following the death of the parent because of the heroic circumstances under which they died. The suddenness and courage of the end seems to justify the means or the errors of the past because to acknowledge otherwise would seem disloyal or disrespectful to their memory. If you dismissed all of the other characteristics and left only "absenteeism", the family qualifies for the diagnosis of "dysfunctional". It is my personal belief that all families could be called that. We are, after all, comprised of fallible human beings and despite our best intentions and efforts, could never totally meet the needs of those entrusted to our care. But the combination of that with a permanent absence of a parent, much less a hero parent whose death always come suddenly and under exceptional circumstances, sets the stage for a high incidence of pain within the family constellation, and hence, "dysfunction". To a large degree the extent of damage depends upon our personalization of the event. Siblings process the loss very differently and their heart response can vary greatly.

So much plays into that individual reaction: defense mechanisms, the proclivity of the personality of the child, the internalized perceptions...that a prediction can never be made decisively about the roles that a child will take to emotionally cope with their pain.

Some of the roles in the hurting family that has become dysfunctional as a result of a precipitating tragedy are consistent and predictable. The ones taken by my siblings and myself were classic and well suited to our respective personalities.

John became the hero. Joan stepped into the "lost child", while Brian assumed the rebel/acting out role. I alternated between hero and mascot, and was the emotional monitor attempting to keep everyone else's issues in check. Brian was probably the most honest in the system. He had the rage of incomplete grief and the deep need for some attention and there was nothing subtle in the way that he chose to express it.

The parts we would play in the family would follow us out of our childhood home into our adulthoods, though the necessity to continue to perpetuate them would no longer exist. We would enter relationships with people and open doors to circumstances that would allow us to continue what was familiar to us and in doing so, perpetuate our own myths that we weren't in pain as a result of a long ago night in April.

For each of us, the children that we were back then went into a type of "hiding" somehow sensing the enormity of the loss and knowing that we would not be getting our needs met. If that realization was there before the loss of my father, I can't say. But I suspect that it might have been that or else the roles we took might not have come so easily to us. A child will adopt whatever it takes to maintain emotional equilibrium. Once they realize that the love that they had hoped for will probably not be, they face a terrifying fork in the road. Either they continue to be in pain for the lack of it or they submerge the need under whatever role can keep them focused and disappear into it. Most chose the latter. We did.

When Joan became "lost", the child decided that life in the external household was too risky and hurtful for her. In typical fashion, to survive her feelings she "left" the premises. She disappeared into herself and into her books where she could escape the reality that now was, and the mother that she found difficult to deal with. She had to find somewhere in which she could thrive as well. Her gifts were her intelligence and her love of independent things, and it turned out that they served her well in her internal haven. She gave up on seeking love in a household that was hostile to her but certainly, didn't give up on the need or desire for it. When she made friends they were with other girls that shared similar issues. Her friends were smart, studious, and invariably, loners that were lost on the periphery of the social scene. They were the "weirdoes" of yesterday the "geeks" of today, that clustered together because they were each other's only option, the only ones that were not picked for the cheerleading teams of the popular girls' lives. They hung out together because it was their last possibility for friendship. It was really that simple. They were lost children too, and they understood each other. Children who have suffered any type of pain within their relationships with others will also seek safe friendships. Joan's friends could find some of the acceptance and love they needed from each other, because their friendships may have served as the ONLY place that they felt connected.

The need of each of them developed an atmosphere of more acceptance. We are more willing to give that which we ourselves hope to get in return. In Joan's case she needed to be accepted, and cared for. She needed to replace the troubled relationship that she had with her mother with some positive female companionship. She didn't want to take the chance of further rejection, so it made all the sense in the world that she would gravitate to girlfriends that were almost certain not to reject her and continue their own isolation. She gravitated towards me, too. I was fairly benign when she would offer to take me places with her, would certainly welcome the opportunity to get out of the house with her. So it worked. Externally. Inside the family it was another issue to harangue her about, and we did and she was.

When Joan got married, my brother said that her bridal party looked like the picture in the dictionary next to "reject". I know it was mean, but I have to say in all fairness that it kind of looked that way. One of her attendants in particular would put her head down and while talking to herself, would walk down the street like a raging bull. How she didn't walk into lampposts I'll never know. Another of them was very rough - the "no stranger to street fights" kind of tough that you really didn't want to tangle with, so when she chose the bridesmaids gowns the other girls declared it "perfect". Go figure. It didn't matter that they were bright red with capes...It seemed like Brian might have something with his observation...the wedding pictures seemed to be of a collection of overweight, overwrought girls looking for all the world, like glandular super-heroes.

Joan would maintain this social proclivity throughout her adult life. Her friends would always be the ones that nobody else seemed to want. They were the odd, needy, strange; often extremely overweight girls that seemed to hang on the periphery. They needed her though, and were safe. And that made all the difference in the world to Joan. If a comparison were to be made with any one of her friends, she would always be the winner. And that in itself would be reason enough for her to have them.

Brian took the rebel role because he could. With his humor and anger and the uncomplicated way he handled emotions with his fists, it was a natural. I think he thrived on it, really. He had the respect that was a requisite for the Carroll men, albeit for a rather perverse reason. He had a channel for the anger that boiled inside of him and he had something that was totally his own that he didn't have to share or compare with John. It was his. And if he couldn't burn down bridges in the academic department like his siblings, he could distinguish himself on the street. He wasn't big but he was feisty, and nothing and no one could keep him out of the middle of some altercation. Being younger, I would absolutely dread the few occasions that my mother would leave me in his care. Invariably, he would run around the apartment turning off all of the lights. Then he would hide and call me to come to where he was.

I would go with my eight-year-old knees knocking through the darkness. THUD!! He would jump down behind me from the top of a door or some piece of furniture. He would laugh himself sick when I screamed like a banshee and scrambled to find the light switch. If he wasn't scaring me out of a few years growth in that manner, he would suddenly decide that it was time for me to learn how to "box". Translation? "It's time for me to smack you around under the guise of teaching you boxing". He would then proceed to rapid-fire headshots until I was either crying from the stinging or from the frustration of not being able to knock him out myself. I remember one time that, for some unknown reason, I was able to get him on the floor and sit on top of him. I flailed at him like a wild woman, crying the entire time. At that very moment, I learned the lesson of revenge, and why you can never get it and why it's not worth it, anyway. As I pummeled him, I was crying because I couldn't seem to hurt him enough...Scary now that I look back, but it was a life lesson I have never forgotten.

I wasn't the only focus of those "object lessons" either. Sometimes it would be some kid who had either hurt me or was suspected of it. Brian would fly in like an avenging angel, and chase the kid for blocks. I never quite knew what happened when he caught him, and that was probably best, but it was a given that he wouldn't bother me again...

And, so it went during his early life. Brian would do what he did best. Sometimes getting busted, sometimes not. And always a wild card. As he got older and the alcohol really started to kick in, his fighting or looking for one would be proportionate with his consumption.

The more he drank the less his inhibition. The less his inhibition the more likely that the rage would blast to the surface, and there would be casualties of the war that was waged within him. It would continue into and through years of his professional life, incongruous with the successes he experienced in his job. By day he was an extremely competent financial advisor but by night, a volatile drunk that could turn nasty in a heartbeat, that was chased by the demons of his past. He would monologue about my father's being absent, the poverty we had to experience, and the abandonment by all of the extended family. He dismissed anything having to do with our Irish heritage as if by separating himself from it he could separate himself from his painful past entirely. He shifted his life goals to the accumulation of money and would spend hours rehearsing how he would go about doing it. The economic disadvantage that we had grown up with had effected him most of all, I think.

Incredibly, he would later visit the same taverns to which my father had gone and drink there too. There was no need for Freud to return to analyze the meaning of that. On some level, he had this love/hate drivenness for the father he barely knew. As much as he needed to find him somewhere, to identify with him in some way, he also needed to reject him for the loss he felt by his absence. It was a tortured search for Brian that sent him squarely to the bottom of a Jack Daniel's bottle.

It is not that unusual for a child who takes the role of rebel to go down that road.

They find early on that they can medicate their feelings by some behavior or substance or lifestyle and that by using it, it can quiet the internal feelings for a time. The problem is that eventually the medicine becomes the sickness and it takes on its own power in the life of the person. The other members who choose to compensate through more acceptable behaviors are similarly using methods to cover their pain, but are less conspicuous, and overtly self destructive. When a person picks up a substance or anything else that eventually owns them they have a larger row to hoe when it comes to recovery. First the medication has to be removed. Then, and only then, can they even begin to deal with the feelings that required the medication or the silencing. It's a long process, indeed. Any therapist with any knowledge of addictions knows this to be true. You cannot heal while there is still a substance that you can retreat behind. Brian eventually came to this knowledge.

He has been sober for many years now. It took the necessary rock bottom. It took his family moving to his aid and spiriting him away and into rehab. It took guts, on his part, and it took guts on ours to override our "loose cannon". He did it though and somewhere in that tough journey was able to face his feelings about the father that never came home from work one long ago night in April. And slowly, he learned forgiveness.

When John stepped into the empty shoes of his father at the age of thirteen it was because he was the most logical, if inappropriate choice. He was the oldest boy.

Already an achiever, already responsible. He had an air of maturity for so young a kid, and because he thought it was his duty and had idolized his father, he won the dysfunctional lottery that was played as soon as the head of household slot was vacated. Within days of the fire he became the resource for my mother, the conduit to the siblings. He was quiet, sad beyond words, and unable to make sense of what had happened, but there he is in the pictures of the funeral holding my mother's arm as he escorted her into the Cathedral. It was a snapshot of what his life would become, and by default, and maybe even reluctantly, he embraced it. In eighth grade. He had no choice.

Probably since the day he raced to tell my father about his accomplishment in getting the scholarship to high school, he had to look forward to his next achievement. With my father gone it would become that much more of a necessity.

He would at least keep up his role for him posthumously. Besides he would have to, in view of the looming financial situation. And he did. And he would. Except for that brief overload issue in his freshman year when he transferred schools, he would push right into one success after another. He would take care of his mother, his family, his business, his wife and daughters, his friends, and anyone else that needed it. He would gain monetary independence, a home in a prestigious town, a law degree…and if he had an edge, a drivenness, it would be understandable, wouldn't it? It wasn't easy barreling from one triumph to another, after all. And it wasn't so easy to push down into yourself all of the anger, resentment, suffering and pain that came after my father's death as you were ushered into a role that was never meant to be yours.

John was the accomplished, paternal keeper of the flame. The family historian. He kept my father's helmet in his office, along with his awards and citations. He catalogued the pictures of the fire, its aftermath and the funeral services. He did it all and if he was irritable or short tempered, he had earned enough respect and awe not to be confronted. And he wasn't. Certainly none of his siblings would risk drawing John's verbal fire. For us he became the human equivalent of Forrest Gump's chocolates. You never knew what you were going to get.

That didn't effect his family standing though, and it stayed that way for years. I remember when he was about sixteen years old and I was six and in kindergarten. I had gone into his room (probably because I was bored) and he worked out for us the encrypted fortune that used to run in the New York Daily News. I can't remember what mine was, but I never forgot his. It turned out to be "rely on self". What made that such a lasting memory for me was not the message per se, but his reaction. He just shook his head with what I would now call a sad, resigned look. I felt bad for him. I wanted him to have mine, which was something benign like "you will have an interesting encounter…"

He seems to have known from the beginning what his role would be. No confusion at all and no chance that something as personal as depression, or anger, or anxiety could relieve him of his responsibilities. No wonder he kept everything locked inside, to be the grist for the mill of his drive.

To those of us that grew up with him and watched him evolve into this wunderkind type of entrepreneur, we knew that along with the pain that festered within him, John spent years in pursuit of my father's acceptance. He wanted and needed to finally feel that he had achieved the "good enough" status that my father withheld, but the tragedy was that he would never know at what point that would have happened. He had to surmise in my father's absence, but since the story had never had an ending back then, it couldn't have one now. He pushed himself to some amorphous limit that he could never quite accomplish. But how he tried was a testimony to his own need to finally make it. He did it all, handled it all. He sought out my father's brothers, and socialized with them often in preference to his siblings.

He could not tolerate any of us berating or criticizing them for their coldness or disinterest in the family of their "beloved" brother. He sought their approval. Major professional successes that they were, I'm certain that he viewed them as a type of replacement for his father, and the acceptance that had never seemed to come from him. A surrogate parentage that in reality never could and didn't exist. I guess he needed some Carroll male to acknowledge his efforts…and by doing so, acknowledge him. Superficially, I suppose they did. After all, he was the only one of us that they ever invited to their functions. We always thought (my brother, sister and I) that it was their token gesture. I still believe that we were right about that.

When John was at the height of his career and thirty-nine years of age; financially secure beyond our best expectations, he suffered a massive heart attack. He didn't die, thank God. He had double bypass surgery. Before too much time had passed though, he was back on the fast track, doing the hero-thing that he did so well. Although frightening, it was only a blip on the screen and business resumed as usual. That close call didn't do much to dampen the fires.   He would still drive himself and maintain his habit of snapping first at whomever he felt had acted stupidly, and thinking later. He also would isolate himself some of the time, and if that need happened to strike him in the middle of a family gathering so be it. He still did all the things he did prior to the surgery, flying around the country, working late, and it was a true blessing that he didn't suffer any more heart crises. He seemed almost nonchalant about his experience, and would say that he was so mentally and spiritually ready that he had actually been half disappointed that he woke up after surgery. I believe he has always had that attitude about his mortality and I can almost understand it. Not only from the spiritual point of view but from the idea that death could offer a rest of sorts from all of the work and responsibility that he had always taken on.   It might even be that it would offer an emotional release. After decades of suppressing pain, the very idea of being set free by oblivion must be welcoming, indeed.

The years would continue to go by, and pretty much the status quo remained intact for him. John would buy and sell a few companies, raise his daughters, travel extensively, and be in touch with us sporadically. As far as his relationship with his siblings, he used to remind me of the nursery rhyme about the girl with the curl in the middle of her forehead. When he was "good he was very, very good, and when he was bad he was horrid". I think that kind of summed up my experiences, and I was sad about that. I missed the young kid who would take me along with him to the basketball courts. The one he was before the stakes and the burdens of heading a family got harder.

Not too long ago and as I mentioned earlier, it seemed that John started to lose some of his abilities for which he was so well known. He began to forget things. Often. He would reach for words sometimes. Repeat himself. He would tell the same story over and over, oblivious to the fact that he had already told it. The diagnosis was alarming for such a young and vital man. He had a disease that would progressively rob him of his faculties. One that would eventually effect his intellectual abilities, acumen and memory.

As for me, I refused to believe it. He was the hero, and in the end of the story, heroes win. They do not fade away and they do not falter. They win. Just like he always did.

Sadly, my wishing does not make it so for him. He is being treated for it but it is only palliative. The truth is that the damage that his system has accrued cannot be reversed. As adults, we all know and can understand what we are hearing. We all have the ability to process the diagnosis and realize the implications. But as the children that we still are deep inside, my siblings and I reject such a notion.

Perhaps as the time evolves, we will be able to merge the different parts of ourselves and come to a type of acceptance. Right now, though, my brother and sister and I still fear losing a "father" for the second time. But we are not unaware, despite our resistance that something wonderful has happened in the course of his illness.

It seems as though he has once again been put in touch with the young boy that he was prior to being rocketed to adult responsibilities. It is as though this condition; this horrible, dreaded state of his body has helped him to reach back over time and capture who he was and could have been had April, 1956 been just another month and year. He has lost that grinding, relentless drive that put him on a hamster wheel of accomplishment that was and would always be "never enough". He has been given a reprieve from chasing the elusive phantoms of his youth and heart. He's nicer. His main focus at this time of his life is simple. He wants to visit shut-ins. He wants to give out of an innocence of heart to those that could use his help. He seems genuinely happy to hear from us when we call and for the first time, we know what we're going to get. Usually the conversation involves a lot of repetition or hesitation, but it doesn't matter at all. He is the unburdened, unencumbered young kid who would still run down to the firehouse if he could. But this time, he wouldn't let the unthinking comment bother him so much. He's the kid who made it big because he could. Not because he had to. He's back to the brother he was before life made him the father that he wasn't. And if it took this to happen; okay. We're just all glad that he's been set free.

And then there was me. Mascot, Emotional watchdog, Golden girl, and Comic relief. I was three. The youngest in the family system often takes the role of family mascot. Probably because as the youngest they automatically qualify as cute, entertaining and a diversion for the rest of the family. I stepped into the slot easily, buffeted by my age and precociousness. I learned that I could make people laugh by being quick on the verbal draw. I learned when I got to school that being the youngest in a group of much older siblings gave me the advantage of knowing things that the other kids didn't. So between those two, I became an excellent student with the added attribute of mischievousness. I worked hard at both and found that for me, laughing at some prank was the stuff that made life worth it. Excellent grades were expected and I produced them. As for the other fun things, well...it was best that that stayed among my friends. My mother was growing more dependent upon my being present for her and resented my getting older and wanting to be with friends. My sister would fuel this fire by telling her that I was going to be wild if she didn't put her foot down. She would and I would figure out some way to get around it. One time I remember is when I discovered the telephone and was in the process of perfecting the art of talking for hours with my friends that lived in the same apartment building. My mother put a small lock on the dial to prohibit our calling out. Undaunted, I called the operator, told her I was blind and asked her to dial for me. My mother could never figure out why her phone bills remained high. This is the kind of stuff that I lived for. It made me laugh, as it did my siblings. And I can say with certainty that we needed it.

I sailed through grade school, got scholarships to high school. Worked at being a waitress to the nuns in the local convent, and would donate ten dollars of my twenty-seven dollar salary to the house. When I got my working papers, I worked for a small supermarket about ten blocks away. I would often save the bus fare and walk knowing that the more I could save, the sooner I could buy myself a dress for the high school dance we usually went to on Saturday night. I wasn't a bad kid at all although I was high spirited and I found the atmosphere of the house I now shared with only my mother not to be conducive to that. I had always found an outlet for my need for adventures with my friends, and later, the boyfriend of the moment. I would take a side trip to the Village, ride the "D" train to the end of the line – stuff that if my mother knew of, would be immediately curtailed. I was grounded once for a year. Honestly, I think that the punishment far outweighed the crime and that the ulterior motive was to keep me around more for company.

So I grew up, went to college. And started my search for a different life where someone would finally take care of me. The mascot role would serve me well in this quest, and did. I found a wonderful young man but was unable to treat him well because I couldn't understand availability.

I ran from everything that represented possibility in my life, and straight into failure. It was a horrendous encounter. Somewhere, I knew that I was looking for the father that I'd lost. I knew that I believed that if I found the exactly right male, in exactly the right package, then I could regain the years that I had missed. I would finally know what safety and security was and the hole in my heart would be finally filled. I even made a list. Older. Financial prospects. Someone that thought I was the best thing he had ever met and would treat me like the treasure I had always wanted to be to someone. I pictured myself working part time. One child, maybe. Maybe not. I would find it hard to have a child having never had the chance to really be one myself. In a way, I had already been a parent to my mother and would like to have time just to be allowed to not have to take care of anyone or anything. Maybe later on then, but not even on the drawing board at present. It's fair to say that this career aspiration often took precedence over my academics. I was majoring in "finding security" and school was merely a means to this end. If most people found their soul mate in college, then I would too. And, so started the arduous journey of poor selections, broken hearts, and disillusionment. I was a dean's list student in trying, though. Over the next years, I tried on many relationships. They all fit the criteria, at least outwardly. They all fit the reality, too. Which was "absenteeism". The dynamics of the relationships became more intense. The ante was always upped. I would try to be whatever it took to gain their conditional love…they would be unable to engage. Any other person who was actually half healthy would not interest me. I was on a mission to recreate what I had known and change the ending. That was the failure I spoke about. I had left the only one that was healthy.

Not too far into my thirties, I decided to utilize all the reading I had done over the years on self-help and psychology, and prepare for a career in mental health. Maybe I could also find solutions for my own angst and discover why I was always on a relationship treadmill. Maybe I could step of it. I headed into a Master's Program, focused on entering private practice. I went through a divorce while finishing up grad school. It was as horrific as they can get. He was the poster boy for "ism"s. Alcohol, women, work, rage, and all in one unavailable package. In other words, the perfect fulfillment of everything I had ever searched for. The only healthy thing about the relationship was its ending.

As a therapist I was a natural. I empathized. And I helped people sort out their problems. I had trained for this since I was a child, after all. Practice boomed, an agency was born, and I finally felt that it was time to revisit my own past for resolution. I did. I learned. I came to understand that deep inside there was a child searching for a father she never got to have. I had spent decades digging through the rubble of a Bronx fire, trying to salvage whatever I could to meet the needs that child. I had piled years of impossible attempts to cope on a pile of unacceptable relationships. I had entered a field to help others in an effort to help myself, and heal the child that woke up with nightmares she couldn't remember. To say it was grueling would be an understatement. To say that it was painful to exhume all of those red herrings of performance, caretaking, and mascotting would not do the recovery justice. It was beyond horrible, even as it was beyond necessary.

I did it though. And in the end, I became a calmer person and a more effective parent. I wrestled myself free from the need to recreate the past as I thought it should have been. Ultimately, if grudgingly, I accepted the most of it for what it was. I still play practical joke, and would tease and torment and set people up so that I can laugh myself silly, but it's different. It's out of a love of fun and not out of a need to escape. I don't keep secrets anymore. Not the ones about family and truth and sadness and what's real. I believe that doing that made us even more damaged than we were after losing my father. The secret of the dysfunctional family is that they keep secrets. They take their pain, hide it in a hall closet, and expect it to stay there as they go about trying to attain normalcy. When the door starts to bulge, they build a larger hallway, but dare not look inside. In doing so, in trying to avert their eyes from the door that threatens to blow open and expose their pain, they burrow deeper into it only to lose themselves in the process. I don't keep secrets anymore. I remember too well what is was like, and of all the places I still want to see, that is not one of them. Not again. Not ever.

CHAPTER ELEVEN

I don't know how it's possible to get through personal loss without some type of spirituality. I don't know what gives people the strength to make sense out of the senseless, or the courage to look life in the eye after their worlds have been shattered by some horrible missile of news that changes life as you have known it. Irrevocably and totally.

No, scratch that. I know it's possible because many members of my family, including myself, did it. In retrospect, it's possible, but I would never advise it. Ever.

Truthfully, I don't know how we did it. I had no frame of reference to give my father's death reason or structure. I had no way to create a construct for it. Later, I would be taught the basics about God. I would be taught about Him, but not about knowing Him. My comprehension of God was vague and the memory verses that were supposed to define my faith were too rote, too sterile. I learned them to get a good grade in religion.

Because my understanding was only surface at best, and devoid of any substantive guidance toward a real relationship with Him, I ended up having no comfort for or acceptance of what had occurred. I found it to be totally irreconcilable that a God that was supposed to have such love for His creation, this distant, amorphous God who maintained such silence, would take someone who was so desperately needed by the family he left behind. It scared me, and like all children who experienced a sudden uncertainty early in their lives, I would forever be waiting for the other shoe to drop. I would live in constant fear of the next loss, the next trauma. I was angry with a God who could watch this happen and concluded that His good will, about which I had been taught in catechism class, was suspect indeed. I mean, how could anyone trust the benevolence of a Being that could watch as a family of children gathered sobbing in a Bronx living room?

As much as I didn't want to have to rely on my own ingenuity, I felt that I had to. As much as I wanted to believe that there was a God, and He had His reasons for the things that happened to us, I ended up thinking that it was an awfully convenient explanation.

Ultimately, it was one that I felt was a little too shrouded in mystery when it involved something as big as my father's death.

I think it would be accurate to say that although I was aware of the existence of God, I was not too enthused about having an ongoing conversation with Him. If He wanted His privacy or secrecy, I thought, He could have it.

It didn't stop my exploration, though. From the time I was about thirteen until well into my thirties, I read whatever I could get my hands on regarding spirituality and faith. Then I started reading psychology as well. It's a safe bet that I was looking for answers for my own pain. While other kids were reading Louisa May Alcott, and L.M. Montgomery, I was delving into books about Buddhism, Protestantism, and Anxiety Management.

Not surprisingly, I also would watch any movie produced that dealt with the theme of someone who had died coming back. I would wait spellbound for the part where the departeds would make themselves known to the living. I would weep with happiness when the characters finally communicated, and even more when they had to part again. Inevitably, the one that had passed away had return to being invisible to the other. But the part that enthralled me was the one in which you knew that the unseen ones kept watch over their living loved ones. I can't describe how much I wanted that to be true.

I really wanted to believe that people could come back to help the ones on earth when they needed it. I think I had to believe it, so as not to feel so utterly deprived of ever having a relationship with my father. It was sad now that I think of it.

In addition, I didn't know what to make of all the emotional, psycho-spiritual information I had gathered. What I needed to believe didn't jive with what seemed to be reality. And apparently, reality wasn't complying with the life theories I was formulating. I had hit an impasse spiritually speaking, but would continue to investigate the emotional and psychological side of things. That worked for a while.

I read my way right into my thirties. By now a professional therapist, and probable humanist if I defined my beliefs contextually. I was okay with that. Psych seemed to respond to a lot of my questions about the present state of individuals, why they became who they did, and what we should do to address their problems. In a way, I think it made me feel a little safer. That life did have explanations, and that the things that happened could be dealt with.

I became able to interpret my client's dialogue and diagnose with consistent accuracy. I would direct therapy towards identifying and restructuring behaviors that caused clients pain. I became quite good at it.

Believing what I did made life seem less chaotic, and I felt better personally and professionally about that. Everything could be explained in one way or another from a psychological perspective. Then my own life went into crisis and theories weren't enough.

I was married to a very successful professional man who was volatile as well as addicted. Alcohol, work, women and rage were his drugs of choice. When it became necessary to leave my home, I did so. Overnight I was without funds, house and friends that we had shared. In the middle of beginning my own practice, I was without any resources. He continued as usual. He employed most of our friends in his business, so they remained. He lived in our house, and within days of my leaving had moved in another woman. He controlled the finances. Although I considered myself the victim, the perpetrator was thriving. For that, no theories applied. It was mind boggling in its injustice.

There is sometimes a pain in life that finds a mark perfectly. That literally takes your breath away with its power. In the process, you are rendered such an incredible injury that you feel it throb deep in your chest. It's how you would feel if someone smashed a sledgehammer right into your sternum and proceeded to pound the same spot repeatedly. I believe that when you feel what I'm talking about, it is really new pain burrowing in and joining with some old one that is already in residence there, and the combination brings you to your emotional knees. With that type of injury, the new heartache seems to have the inside track on exactly how to "locate and merge"- almost like an emotional missile. It's like that's the only viable place that it can go, and it gives new strength to old pain as it explodes into your chest. I had felt that physical pain before. It is believed that we actually can feel painful sensations in parts of our bodies that we associate with the trauma. The classic

"Pain in the neck", "Weight on my shoulders" phenomenon, where the individual is actually feeling in their body how their mind interprets the emotional conflict. I had felt that chest pain when something had deeply hurt my feelings, when someone I loved had been cruel, or when the situation involved loss of some kind. It was an old, unresolved reservoir of hurt that could be tapped in the present. It was the pain of my heart breaking…again.

That was the way it was for me this time, too. I couldn't comprehend the absolute callousness of a person you had trusted. I was without words, resources, or plans. I was at the end of my self, despite the training in the human psyche. I wanted to die, figuratively and literally. If this was the way life was going to be, I had had enough.

The sledgehammer had done its work. It had hit the mark with an accuracy and constancy that I cannot adequately describe. Suffice it to say, that the physical pain almost bent me in half in its intensity. I thought I would die. I wanted to die. I remember thinking that of all the things that I had had to adjust too in my life, this was beyond the pale and I was incapable and unwilling to do it.

I was absolutely convinced that I would not survive this emotionally. I had so missed the mark that I had trusted a man who had the capability of discarding his marriage within hours of acting out his own rageful behavior. The consummate abandonment.

I had seen him do similar things to long-term employees, friends that disagreed with him, young people that he trained in his profession. But of course, I held the misguided belief that it would be different with me.

That I would "change the ending" and this time this unavailable, out of control addict type personality would never leave, or risk my leaving him. I needed a male relationship to finally be something I could depend on and had bet the wrong hand. He was incapable. He was when we had met. He was cruel and self absorbed, and given to violence. He always had been. In other words, he was the perfect choice for someone who had once felt abandoned.

C.S. Lewis called pain the "great megaphone of God"...(1) And, I totally believe it. When I had no place else to go, when logic and education and humor and people failed me, I made a last ditch effort. I called upon God to help me and He did.

Paul of Tarsus was a persecutor of Christians whom was chosen by God to be the apostle to the Gentiles. The start of his conversion began quite dramatically when he was thrown from his horse and heard the voice of Christ. Before he resumed his journey, or took another step from his position on the ground, his life was inexorably changed. If I can be so bold as to make the comparison, I know how he felt.

I cried out to God and He met me with extravagant love in return. He didn't seem to care how cynical I had been. He didn't seem to mind how I had negated Him in favor of "rational" thought and explanation. Simply, God showed up. I knew it more than I ever knew anything else in my life. I called out, He answered. I returned as a prodigal, and He ran out to meet me. I knew it. I was not crazy; I was not doing some wishful thinking. I was no longer in physical pain. That knife that had been sticking in the center of my chest was pulled out, wiped off, and although the wound remained, the patient would survive. I truly believe that God took and used this horrible situation to bring me to a place of helplessness. I could not rely on my intellect, my education, my former support network, or myself. I was at the end of my own resources, and that put me squarely at the beginning of His. I read another book entitled, "Trusting God "by Jerry Bridges. It spoke to some of my long held questions. I read "Reasons Skeptics Should Consider Christianity" by Josh McDowell, and miraculously, it made sense from a logical and empirical standpoint.

I visited the church of my childhood, but inherently knew that this search would not lead back there for me. I visited a friend's church, and was touched by the simplicity of the message, the people, the Gospel.

Stripped of religion, the idea of a personal God who wept with us and Who didn't author bad things in our lives...Who wanted a personal relationship with us...Who was crazy about us...drew me like nothing had previously. I studied the Bible, I spoke with Christians, and I saw it in an entirely new light, with entirely new eyes. And, I embraced it. For all those long years, I had missed the message, concentrating on the messengers. I had dismissed their enthusiasm, their simplicity as being, well...simple.

If that was the explanation for this awakening sense of comfort and purpose, if in simplicity could be found comfort as well as eternity, I would commit to it, follow it and adopt it. God had broken through to me at the absolute end of myself, and showed me His home. I liked it better than any one I had ever lived in before, and decided to stay. We're both very happy.

It has been years now. I still feel the same. I struggle with the understanding of God the Father, loving and merciful and so intricately involved in our everyday life. I struggle because I don't have anything to relate it to; I have no frame of reference.

CHAPTER TWELVE

The purpose of this writing came out of a desire born of personal loss. My intention was to offer help and hope to those who have survived a hero. It is a different type of survival that begs so many questions that it is distinguished from other more natural deaths of loved ones. To lose someone who has died in service to others leaves those they have left behind with questions that are uniquely particular to a hero's death. Often, conflicting emotions wage a war that many fear expressing for fear that any negativity they may feel would be disrespectful or disloyal to the person they have lost. You may even (like I did) wonder why your husband, wife, brother, or child chose the actions they did knowing they risked losing their life, and in so doing, losing you with it. Could they have been so driven by duty and honor that they put that over everyone who loved them? Could they have so consumed by their desire to do the right thing at the right time, that they would risk their very presence in those lives that depended upon them? And why did they go forward when everything reasonable would have advised retreat? "Why?" we ask to the empty place at the table, and then feel shame at our very question. "Why?" we ask God, and strain to hear something, anything that could make even the least bit of sense to us. I never got an answer. I could never even fathom an answer that would have comforted me, or silenced my heartfelt need for some understanding of the loss that we suffered.

Maybe that is not for the living to know. But, I never stopped asking. Neither will you, if the truth be told.

Growing up in the shadow of a hero has its own set of questions and doubts. It requires things of a person that transcend their ability to comprehend. It calls for public acceptance and displays of pride, when the truth of it is that you want to disassociate yourself from those things that seemed responsible for pillaging your life and robbing you of your loved one for a greater cause. Growing up or adjusting to life without a hero brings its own complexities. If you had issues with the loved one, or relationships were strained, or you were privy to their darker side that the public would never see, it feels like scandal to reveal these things to anyone. It feels uncomfortable to even think them and before too much time passes, you may come to doubt your perceptions.

Or if you don't doubt yourself, you may hide your true feelings, burying them away in deference to the larger picture of the heroism.

If your husband or father or wife or child had his/her own difficulties, or if your relationship with them was volatile, or tense or disappointing...you may leave it unprocessed and unhealed rather than explore the negative aspects of the person that is so widely applauded. Confusion may obscure your feelings as the reality that everyone else recalls is not the one in your memory. Or, you may minimize your own feelings about the relationship, and emotionally "sell yourself out" in an effort to preserve the image.

What can we do for ourselves? What can we do for the children who cannot understand that any cause could be worth sacrificing their father or mother to, and wonder why their parent had to take the chance on not being there to see them grow up.

Children don't really understand the danger involved in service occupations. They know that their Mommy or Daddy is a firefighter, or a policeman, or an astronaut, but primarily they know them as the men and women that come home most of the time to tuck them in. They don't know the dangers, until one night they are told that their parent is not coming home, and that they are now a hero. They don't understand that, and often, the adults that are left to care for them don't understand it either.

SUGGESTIONS FOR ADULT
SURVIVORS OF HEROES

1.   Talk about it. All of it. The good, the bad, and everything in between.

After the initial shock of the loss, there invariably comes a time when life settles into a semblance of the routine it will now take on. The relatives have left, the ceremonies are concluded. The pace of life that had stopped abruptly, slowly insinuates itself into your awareness. But for you, loss remains ever present and incomprehensible. You may think that to express your feelings would be redundant, or burdensome on your listeners.

You may think that you are expected to honor your absent loved one with a stoic silence that serves as a testimony to the rightness of their sacrifice. You may imagine that you no longer have any words that haven't been thought, said or swallowed. You may along with a daily crushing grief, have anxiety about what you are supposed to do now. Really your priority is not supporting other people at this time, but to do whatever you need to do to begin to recover.

However small a step, however selfish it may seem, you have to somehow take care of yourself. The instructions that are given by all airline personnel on all flights are the ones that you have to remember. In case of emergency in the flight cabin, oxygen masks drop from the ceiling. You are instructed to put the mask on your own face FIRST before you attend to others. The reasoning is clear. You would be unable to aid anyone else. If you were oxygen deprived and needed to offer assistance to others you would be unable to do so, and everyone would be in even further jeopardy. Even so, the principles apply to emotional healing and well being. You have just suffered a life crisis of enormous proportion. To not equip yourself, and ready yourself to administer support to others in your sphere, puts all of you in danger. To be able to function and to pick up the pieces of a former life you must have the capacity to do so. It means a tough walk through your own issues that have been precipitated by the loss, and often that takes expression. The anger and anxiety...the fear, the loss not expressed, in its enormity cannot be dismissed.

It burrows down and finds a home and surfaces in the everyday activities of the life that you must resume. The confusion, the anger, the helpless sense of loss needs expression, and it is best done with trusted friends, or counseling. Allow yourself to be angry. Even at the person that you have lost. It will not last forever, nor will it be an exercise in either disloyalty or futility.

Allow yourself to be where you are emotionally at any given time. It is a process that takes time, and it is a draining one. But, there is no standard time or manner in which to grieve. There are no parameters that are universal. They are yours alone, and yours to experience at whatever pace and by whatever means you can.

2. GIVE YOURSELF PERMISSION TO FEEL THE
    ENTIRE SPECTRUM OF EMOTIONS.

Far better to voice whatever it is you're feeling, than to have it submerge and morph into ongoing depression. If you feel uncomfortable in the beginning, or cannot manage the words, write them. Write them in a letter form. Write them to the lost loved one. Sometimes it's easier to write in letter form that which we may decide to destroy than it is to journal our feelings. You may feel awkward about diarying or journaling, and that's okay, too. But the act of writing a letter is something familiar. Do it. It will help prevent losing track of what the true issues were and what they are.

They change, you know. They leap back and forth across time, and are above the laws of reason. They are not respectful of place or company. They are real and they demand an audience. Let yourself spend time with them. Perceived right now as intruders, they will one day become your friends. They will be a part of the healing process. Not only that, but it helps you to understand the need to own them and express them and in doing so, you become more understanding.

Write over and over. Talk with someone who is aware that it is not their task to comfort you by well-meaning sentiments such as "you'll be alright", or "it may hurt right now, but…" Admittedly, they are trying to help, but may be too uncomfortable as a witness to your pain and need for you to be better before you are able. Don't allow yourself to be silenced by another person's discomfort. The stakes are too high for you.

Talk to your family, too. It is not harmful to openly discuss your feelings with children, as long as the substance of your talk is age appropriate. Children feel more validated in their own feelings if they see their parent modeling self acceptance. My own mother was not able to do this.

She externalized her emotions in many ways, via anxieties or physical ailments, but was always unable to share anything but anger with us. She transferred her need to feel supported to my older brother, and without words, began a dynamic that would last throughout his life.

It is interesting to speculate how that could have turned out differently, had she chosen the road of exploring her own feelings first and sharing with us later. I believe that our lives would have developed quite differently. But her inability to heal herself gave us the family tradition of keeping our emotions inside and taking on our respective roles to compensate.

It started (or continued) the rule of keeping the family secrets, which of course was the result of her not tending to her own. When the elephant came in the front door and settled in the living room, her only way to cope was to ignore it and bid us do likewise. We chose to step around it ever mindful of its presence, but hoping not to frighten the other siblings or my mother by referring to it. Her secrets involved abject fear of being left on her own with children, with little money and fewer prospects. Had she shared that with other adults I wonder how much different she would have been, and how much more tolerant of her children's human flaws.

I am not suggesting that any adult should speak to children as contemporaries, certainly. I am equally not advocating total divesting of all feelings, without regard to content, to children, or using them as surrogate spouses.

I am simply encouraging dialogue that addresses family pain and grief and whatever other feelings, and allowing all of it to be acceptable. If necessary and if more help is needed, seek professional help for the family. Bringing one of the children can make the child think that they alone are abnormal. On top of their grief, this self-definition can be devastating. Go to therapy as a family and participate as individuals in a system that has sustained tremendous loss…together.

3.   ENLIST HELP

I am not speaking of the psychological and spiritual kind here. This is the type of practical assistance that acknowledges your lack of readiness to jump back into normal routine prematurely. Often we underestimate the demands on our bodies that a great emotional toll extracts. We seek the familiar. We so want to feel "normal". And there is nothing wrong with that at all.

But, if we are truly not up to it, if we need to take time to just stop and feel, it can add to the burden of adjustment for both body and soul. We want to believe that any blow that we receive to our mind and spirit is less visible than to our bodies, and therefore lesser in importance. We tell ourselves that our loved ones need our strength, and so try to muster a bravery that we do not feel.

Don't add to your burden. All of your responsibilities, all of your routines will be there when you have gathered the true strength you need. You cannot give anything from an empty tank. Refilling any emotional reserve will have to happen first. Minimizing your own pain to attend to others will take place at some time but for now, the larger courage lies in feeling and standing in your own loss for a time. Which is why we often need the physical assistance, presence and efforts of others to handle our practical lives for a while. Handle yourself as you would a friend who had just had surgery. You would not expect them to leap from their bed and act as they would normally just after being operated on. At first they progress from the bed to a chair to standing. When they try to walk, it is for short distances with assistance. Gradually, the lengths they can walk become longer, until they can go home for more recovery and rest.

There is little difference between you and them during the initial stages of loss. Treat yourselves accordingly and put no demands on yourself that require you to spring back into your routine after the major emotional surgery you have just experienced.

WHEN THERE ARE CHILDREN

1. DON'T TELL THEM ANYTHING BUT THE TRUTH

Sometimes a parent worries about telling a child the truth about what has happened to their other parent, grandparent, or relative. They believe that the concept of death is too difficult for a child to understand or that it will unduly frighten them. In their well-meaning efforts, they may use euphemisms for death such as "Your daddy went away." or "God took your Daddy". For children, who take things they hear very literally, they construe this to mean exactly what is said. "Went away" leaves a child wondering if or when they will be back.

"God taking them" makes for confusion and fear that God could take them too, and that people simply disappear at the whim of the Almighty. Of course we should design our language to accommodate a child's ability to understand, but not in favor of the truth. They may not be able to grasp the finality, or the essence of what you are saying in total, but an age appropriate explanation is really the best approach. Leave out the details that are not necessary. When my uncle told me about my own father and the manner in which he died, it was too much and too abstract for me to comprehend at the age of three. I feared that our apartment building would similarly fall down on us, and had nightmares nightly for years. I truly remember myself trying to process the thought of "death". I remember being frustrated, and not finding the word "death" an adequate resolution to his permanent "goneness". But, I would with time, and that would have been adequate without graphic details.

2. REASSURE YOUNGER CHILDREN THAT THEY HAD NOTHING TO DO WITH IT

Children are the center of their own universe. Under the age of eight, for example, many times they display aspects of "magical thinking."

A small child really believes that he/she has special capabilities to bring things about. If the rhyme says" Step on a crack, break your mother's back", the child will truly believe that they can bring harm upon their mother by inadvertently stepping on the crack. They are literal thinkers. They believe that magical powers are real as well, and accessible to and by them.

Sometimes in their egocentricity, a little one will think that their parent or grandparent will not come home because they did something to make them leave. They didn't do a task that they were asked to do, they were not nice, obedient...the list could be exhaustive. Reassure them that there was absolutely nothing that they could have done and that they did nothing to cause this loss. Tell them that they were loved so much by the other parent from the day they were born that he/she would never have dreamed of leaving.

Communicate to them that although the parent will miss all of the family members deeply, he is happy where he is and will wait to see him/her again. Say this more than once. It helps to know that the parent will miss him/her too.

3.   ALLOW THEM TO EXPRESS WHATEVER FEELINGS THEY HAVE

Children, like adults, will experience emotions that seem to change suddenly. They may vacillate from crying to appearing out of sorts. They may get nasty with other kids, or hard to handle for their caretakers. They may revert to more childlike behaviors, as well. It is not unusual for a child that has suffered any type of trauma to revert to thumb sucking, bedwetting, or incontinence. Younger children may fear not having the surviving parent in their sight. Older ones may recluse themselves more. Throughout my own childhood I was petrified at the thought of my mother dying. So much so that I would cry every year on New Years Eve. My family believed it was because I was very sentimental, and I let them think that. The truth was that I was afraid of the coming year and its uncertainty. I knew that we had made it through the last year without her dying, but was unsure about the coming one. I kept that pattern right up until her death when I was twenty-two.

Nightmares are not uncommon, nor are new fears or night terrors.

Even a young child may feel that they now have to be more of a "grown up" for mommy or daddy.

They may make gestures that appear more adult in an effort to step into the role that has been vacated. Children may even try to act as if everything is normal, and that they are quickly recovered despite the initial trauma. They may even act annoyed when questioned regarding how they are doing.

Their reactions are unique, many and varied. Children often exhibit some or most of these symptoms over time. As the surviving caretaker it is important for you to understand that they are trying to cope with all of the emotional unrest that they are experiencing. They have to assimilate horrific news, major life changes, and family grief all in a brief time period and their world has literally been shattered. They are trying, to the best of their

171

somewhat limited ability, to piece this new puzzle back together but need all the sensitivity we can give them while they struggle to do so. Giving them the safety and freedom to express their grief when they want to and the understanding and space when they do not, is the most productive thing that we can do for them.

4.   DON'T TALK IN FRONT OF THEM AS IF THEY ARE NOT THERE.

Children, although small in stature and sometimes not observed, often seek the company of adults in the aftermath of family trauma.

They need the inclusion and the closeness, as well as the assurance that they still have a place in the family constellation although the family itself has changed drastically. Often, we forget their presence as we engage in adult conversation with other family members or friends or visitors. We may say things that are not age appropriate for the children. Talking about personal details of our lives or worries or burdens may lead the child to conclude things that were not meant. A child does not have the resources to process things as objectively as we think that we might be stating them. Additionally, they have that tendency to somehow write themselves into whatever scenario they are hearing. For a mother or father to refer to their fears about money, for example, may result in the kids feeling like a burden. (I know it did in our family.) For a parent to speak about the child's reaction and their worries about their abilities to cope with the death in front of the child can be embarrassing to the child, and they will take care not to show these emotions and internalize instead.

I remember going to the butcher shop with my mother soon after my father died. She spoke quite openly with the man behind the counter about how I was dealing with his death. I was three, but I understood the conversation and was self-conscious about expressing my feelings from that point on.

As much as a child needs to feel included, valuable and part of the family and the changes that are taking place, they need to be excluded from some of the more adult or observational things that the parent is processing and discussing.

5.   EVENTUALLY, BRING A MALE/FEMALE
        ROLE MODEL INTO THEIR LIVES.

Not right away certainly, but sometime during the first year, find a "surrogate" parent for the children to relate to. I'm not speaking about a boyfriend, or romantic partner. I'm talking about some person who would agree to spend some one on one time with each child on a regular basis.

The purpose of this is to expose the child to the particular insight and perspective, as well as relationship, that an opposite sex adult can offer. Children need to have the balance of a male/female influence. Someone in the family, an uncle or grandfather, an aunt or grandmother or even someone from the church family can provide the role model that the most well meaning parent cannot. There is a place for gender specific activities and quality time that has been vacated that truly needs to be filled. Both boys and girls can benefit from a relationship with an adult male that is nurturing, safe and special.

When my siblings and I were growing up, we had only one uncle that would even come close to this surrogate type relationship with us. Unfortunately, he passed away while we were all still quite young and there was never a replacement for him. Perhaps that would have changed things for us. A male figure that we could have observed and had some type of unique relationship with may well have changed many of our future choices. For my sister and I, it might have revealed what appropriate treatment was from a male in our lives.

For my brothers, they may have felt less of a burden to head the family, or refuse to, as it turned out. Someone who had shown Brian that he cared, or someone that could model for John something other than drive and work would have indeed, made a powerful difference.

As for church members, it is my personal belief that men in the church with families need to extend themselves to children that are left without a father. Similarly, women share the same responsibility to be a presence in families that have lost a mother. If we fail to do this for these children, there should be absolutely no surprise if the children later show a lack of interest in the church, or of the things of God. We would have only ourselves to blame. Children would understandably not choose to engage in a church family that they never knew.

Catherine Carroll-Parker, Ph.D., M.S.W.

I know that we felt that way. We went to church and saw other fathers with their families who would ask about us but not offer to engage. It truly gave us a sense of isolation that for me, at least, was never breached. If there are no volunteers in that arena, ask. The worst case is that you will need to continue your search elsewhere.

Adults that do not respond to the needs of children make no difference as to whether the child continues to need or not. The child has someone missing in his/her life, and has a void that needs to be addressed. Explain to the child that a new person is not a replacement for their parent. Otherwise, they would not venture into the relationship for fear of "forgetting" him/her.

This individual is a "friend", and the purpose of this relationship is solely and exclusively for the child, never the adult. Approach presenting the time they would spend together as the other person's request. It restores the child's need for specialness that they would be so noticed and could promote their willingness to participate.

If there were more than one adult that would be willing to develop a tie with the child that would work too. One word of caution: choose someone that you identify with as an adult. Their values, their worldview, their approach to God, families and life in general. You need to know the type of person well that you entrust your child to. Don't let that scare you off, it only requires knowing the person.

6. NEVER, EVER TRY TO SEPARATE THE CHILD FROM THEIR HERO PARENT

Even if you think that the child is spending too much time talking about, handling objects that belonged to their parent, reminiscing, or fantasizing, don't disallow their need to do so.

They are creating a past, a history of the parent that is no longer there. They are trying to commit to memory the parent that is gone. They may be grieving over their loss and to admonish them would not address the issues but submerge them.

By spending time there the child is saying something. They are trying to either remember, or feel the closeness that they are afraid will go away. Even as their parent did. Encourage them to talk about what they are feeling. Ask them if there is anything that they need. Usually they can tell you. If not, keep encouraging them.

Understand that you can meet some of their needs but there will be a bond with the child and his hero that he will always need to honor. That does not mean either that we glorify the parent, or paint a picture that is grander than the person ever could have been. It is simply that we allow the child to have his bond, never disparage the parent (whatever your own issues might have been with him/her), and listen closely to what the child is saying by his efforts to connect. If you fear that it is extreme, or much too time consuming and is in any way harmful to the child, then a consult with a professional as a family may be indicated. As a parent who knows their child, I believe that you will know if this is necessary.

And finally, allow time. In the early days of grief, it is a constant. Over time, the thousand times a day that we think of the person becomes hundreds…and then dozens.

7.   ALLOW TIME

Time has to do its work on the shock, the sorrow and the readjustment.   Although studies speak of an emotional adjustment period of being two to five years, I think we can allow that there is no set time and no specific manner in which we process such loss.

It is as individual as those that have to do it are, and as unique as each of them are. It is a part of life this part of death, and one that requires every ounce of courage that we have.   It is also a pain that fades but does not resolve completely, as long and as wide as love; and it resides in some part of us always.

When we lose a hero, it is somehow different. We loved them, certainly, but the world loves them with us, which feeds and validates our own loss all the more. Perhaps the survivors are heroes, too then.

Even if they themselves did not walk into a burning building. Even if they were not aboard a space shuttle, or dedicate themselves to keeping the peace or the crime rate down. Even if they were the unknown faces in the crowd of mourners. Maybe we were heroes too. Maybe we, the families, shared in their bravery by giving the ones that took the front lines a safe place to come home to. I hope that. I believe that. I truly do.

CHAPTER THIRTEEN

The world has become an increasingly uncertain place. Wars and rumors of wars, the ongoing threat of terrorist attacks, urban sprawl, an escalation in crime. With that comes the likelihood that there will be a greater need for the individuals that seek to make a difference, to walk into places that would make the rest of us cringe. These men and women have reached down into themselves and found a greater purpose. They are not fearless but they will overcome that fear by the dedication that they feel to a larger cause. One that supercedes their human frailties and calls them to risk their very lives for the chance to provide others with security, freedom and a life worth living.

Across time, these men and women have taken our place on the front lines of danger. They have stepped into fires, run across battlefields, taken on criminals, and helped each other down stairwells in smoke filled towers. They have run forward when they could have turned and fled. They have stood their ground when retreat would have been the better part of wisdom.

And they have fallen. In numbers too vast to count. But when they did, others rose up and took their places. It has always been the way. Despite a human's frailties and frequent insensitivities to his fellow man, there has never been a shortage of heroes. I wish it were not so. I wish that there never existed the need to put our finest and best into a position that would rob us of their presence. I wish that for myself and for anyone that has ever experienced someone coming to their door with the news of their widowhood or their fatherlessness.

But I know that without these men and women, without their sacrifice, we would be defenseless against the dangers in our world.

So I thank them. I thank them for their sacrifice and their courage. I thank them for dedicating themselves to keeping us safe, but I can't help but wish that it wasn't necessary.

To them, then.

May they go with God.

SONG FOR A HERO

Watching you dress and go as before,

Your uniform lying there,

Pressed on the door

Quietly summoning; whispering lore

Of all of the heroes that wore it before,

And you listen, and hear them, and it all feels so right

While I hold my old pillow

And pray "not tonight…"

Your face is filled with strength and pride,

Your hat set defiant, a bit to the side

And despite my fears, the ache inside

I soften and smile and try to hide

My worry that someday your luck will run out

And I'll never know why

I'll always have doubts

Whether courage or folly brought it about.

You spend your nights rescuing lives

All of your life you've fought and you've strived

Catherine Carroll-Parker, Ph.D., M.S.W.

To be a hero, a man…

A savior of sorts

A man among men, who couldn't be bought

And you're there, and you've done it,

You're winning your fight,

But I'll hold my old pillow,

And pray "not tonight…"

So, be cautious my hero,

Be careful, if brave;

I can't stand with your captains

And weep at your grave

I'll love you and watch you stand straight with your pride

And help you to follow the dreams that you ride,

I 'll be here for always

But late in the night,

I will hold my old pillow

And pray "not tonight"…

Written by: Catherine Carroll- Parker, 1980

GOODBYE FOR NOW

And there will come a time

When I'll see your face

And I'll hear your voice

And there we will laugh again

And there will come a day

When I'll hold you close

No more tears to cry

'Cause we'll have forever

But I'll say goodbye...for now

Corner of Eden Album, K. Trocolli

c. 1998 Sony/ATV Songs LLC

Catherine Carroll-Parker, Ph.D., M.S.W.

BIBLIOGRAPHY

Bridges, Jerry. (1991). TRUSTING GOD. Colorado: Navpress.

Lewis, C.S. (2001). MERE CHRISTIANITY. Michigan: Zondervan.

McDowell, Josh. (1986). REASONS SKEPTICS SHOULD CONSIDER CHRISTIANITY.
Illinois: Tyndale House.

Catherine Carroll-Parker, Ph.D., M.S.W.

ABOUT THE AUTHOR

Dr. Catherine Carroll-Parker is a survivor of a hero. She is also a therapist, educator and conference speaker who specializes in Dysfunctional Families. With years of professional experience in individual and family counseling, she tells her personal story of coping with sudden loss and offers help to anyone that has ever been touched by this type of tragedy. It is written from the heart, and it is written from experience to all of us that ever had to process things such as 9-11, war or high danger occupations.

Catherine has two grown children and lives in Maryland with her husband, Dan.